2nd Edition

Berklee Jazz Keyboard Harmony

Using Upper-Structure Triads

To access audio visit:
www.halleonard.com/mylibrary
Enter Code
"1383-7081-7971-5333"

Suzanna
Sifter

Berklee Press

Editor in Chief: Jonathan Feist
Vice President of Online Learning and Continuing Education: Debbie Cavalier
Assistant Vice President of Operations for Berklee Media: Robert F. Green
Assistant Vice President of Marketing and Recruitment for Berklee Media: Mike King
Dean of Continuing Education: Carin Nuernberg
Editorial Assistants: Yousin Choi, Martin Fowler, Emily Goldstein, Emily Jones, Amy Kaminski, Andrea Penzel, Jacqueline Sim
Cover Design: Kathy Kikkert

ISBN 978-0-87639-154-9

Berklee
Press

1140 Boylston Street
Boston, MA 02215-3693 USA
(617) 747-2146

Visit Berklee Press Online at
www.berkleepress.com

Berklee Online

Study music online at
online.berklee.edu

DISTRIBUTED BY

HAL•LEONARD®
7777 W. BLUEMOUND RD. P.O. BOX 13819
MILWAUKEE, WISCONSIN 53213

Visit Hal Leonard Online
www.halleonard.com

CONTENTS

ACKNOWLEDGMENTS

Thanks to Debbie Cavalier for her initial belief in this project; Jonathan Feist for his patience and hard work to get the text out; Hal Crook for introducing me to USTs when I was a Berklee student; Tom McKinley for his inspiring lessons during my studies at New England Conservatory; Charlie Banacos for teaching me USTs and US clusters for two years straight!; Tony Germain and Stephany Tiernan for their support of my UST class; the students of my UST classes for their great energy and inspiration; Rob Rose for his leadership as producer of the recordings; John Lockwood, Casey Scheuerell, and Dino Govoni for their great musicianship.

This book is dedicated to my mother, Magdalene Liptay, who has so supported my performing and teaching careers, over the years.

FOREWORD

The heart of Berklee College of Music's approach to teaching jazz piano has always revolved around the intense study of harmony, reharmonization, and voicings. We stress the use of high level, high degree tension voicings, including but not limited to voicings in fourths, clusters, upper-structure triads, and other types of polychords.

Needless to say, great composers use a variety of these types of voicings. Familiarity with them helps to improve our ears, causing familiarity of new sounds and reinforcement of harmonic knowledge and experimentation. In the process of learning and performing the upper-structure triad voicings, there is an added benefit resulting in expanded improvisational lines, for these voicings can be used both vertically and linearly.

Suzanna Sifter has taken these concepts and expanded on them, first in her popular courses and private lessons at Berklee, and now, in this book.

If you practice these concepts and exercises, you will greatly improve your understanding and musicianship, as a jazz pianist. I urge you to invest your time in this approach. Your ears will thank you!

Tony Germain
Assistant Chair, Piano Department
Berklee College of Music

THE TRIADS

Jazz piano voicings are known for their rich, vibrant harmonic sound. These colors come from adding tensions to seventh chords. Seventh chords usually contain at least one tension; however, multiple tensions are often used to color a seventh chord.

These tension combinations can be organized into triads with a mixture of chord tones and tensions. Triads are a great way of organizing tension combinations in jazz piano voicings. The two kinds of triads used throughout this book are called *lower-structure triads* (LSTs) and *upper-structure triads* (USTs). LSTs are comprised of chord tones, while USTs contain a combination of chord tones and tensions (one to three tensions).

The rule here is that a UST must contain at least one tension. While some texts require all notes of the triad to be tensions in order to be called a UST, the definition used here is that a UST must have *one or more tensions.*

The LSTs and USTs used in this book are traditional triad qualities: major, minor, augmented, or diminished. In this text, the seventh degree of any chord is considered a chord tone, not a tension.

In order to find the LSTs and USTs of a seventh chord, you will stack triads (two adjacent thirds) on each note of the chord scale. This makes the definition of an LST any traditional triad that is made up of only chord tones (1, 3, 5, and 7). The LSTs will always be built on the root and third of the chord. (Note that some USTs appear on roots and thirds as well.)

USTs are built on scale degrees where traditional stacked triads contain one or more tensions, such as any type of 9, 11, or 13. The LSTs and USTs are named as the Roman numeral of the scale degree. This Roman Numeral method allows for quick memorization of tensions and ease of transposition of any given UST based from the root of any primary chord. For example, Roman numeral V is G over CMaj7(9), and F over B♭Maj7(9). The tensions depend on the seventh chord quality, chord scale, and placement in the harmonic progression.

USTs are played in the RH on top of "chord sound," generally the guide tones (3 and 7) plus one other note (9, 5 or 13) in the LH. The guide tones express the chord quality, while the UST adds color.

Throughout this text, we will study each seventh chord quality with various chord scales, which will result in a large variety of LSTs and USTs. You will find a multitude of options and combinations of tensions to significantly expand your comping palette.

We will study each seventh chord quality one at a time by choosing a chord scale to find the LSTs and USTs that will be placed above left hand voicings in order to create full-sounding jazz piano voicings. We will study all traditional seventh chord qualities: major 7, dominant 7, minor 7, minor 7♭5, and diminished 7. In chapter 6, we will explore alternate scales of the dominant 7 chord, which come from parent scales other than major. In chapter 7, we will apply the knowledge and sounds of USTs harmonically for jazz comping in the II V I progression, as most standard progressions in the "American Songbook" include many II V I progressions.

You will discover how USTs can be used as an organized method of adding rich sounding textures to jazz piano voicings.

SCALE ANALYSIS

All scales are compared to the major scale (Ionian mode) and written with accidentals. For example, the Lydian mode is written 1 2 3 ♯4 5 6 7, with the accidental reflecting the variance from the parallel major scale.

Every chord quality has corresponding chord scales, which you can determine based on the chord symbol and harmonic context.

Chord Symbols

In this book, the relationship between chord symbols, chord qualities, and tensions is specific. If I intend, for example, a 9,♯11 to be in a CMaj7 chord, I will write CMaj7(9,♯11). In jazz charts, such as fake books, tensions are often left out. It is understood that the performer can make the decision about which tensions to add for a richer sound. For the sake of clarity and guidance, I always specify what tensions should be included. These tension-specific chord symbols, played as USTs, are played in the right hand (RH).

IN BLUE

1

As an introduction to how using USTs sound, please listen to "In Blue," the first audio track. I composed "In Blue" in honor of one of the great developers of USTs in jazz harmony, Bill Evans. The chord progression is based on "Blue in Green," written by Miles Davis, yet is clearly influenced by the harmonic sense of Bill Evans. The melody of "In Blue" is harmonized with USTs, performed as a solo piece. Listen to the rich harmonic vocabulary, which will soon be yours as you make your way through this book!

In Blue
for Bill Evans

Fine

CHAPTER 1

Major 6/7

In this chapter, we will learn to use upper-structure triads (USTs) with major 7 chords. Suggested standards for practicing major 7 chord USTs are "Very Early," "If You Never Come to Me," "Inner Courage," and the bridge of "Night and Day."

CHORD SCALE

To discover the USTs of a major 6/7 chord, first choose its corresponding chord scale—typically, the major scale (Ionian mode) or the Lydian mode.

For a major 6/7 chord without specified tensions, use the major scale, where the chord's root, major 3rd, perfect 5th, major 6th, and major 7th correspond to the scale degrees 1, 3, 5, 6, and 7. The 2 is interpreted as tension 9, and the 4 (11) is not an available tension because it conflicts with the 3, and is thus called an "avoid note."

Fig. 1.1. C Major Scale with Chord Tones, Tensions, and the Avoid Note

Lydian, the fourth mode of the major scale, is another good choice as a chord scale of major 6/7, because its I chord is also a major 7 chord. Lydian is used when the major 7 chord contains specified tensions (9,♯11) or (9,♯11,13).

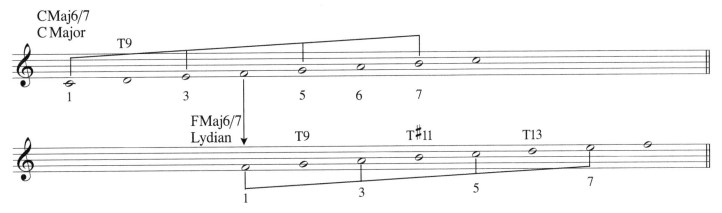

Fig. 1.2. C Major and F Lydian with Tensions

Practice 1.1. Learning Major 6/7 Chords and Associated Scales

While it's helpful to practice exercises in all keys, a good place to start is the keys of C, F, B♭, E♭, and G.

1. Practice all major 6/7 chords in all inversions.

2. Set a metronome to quarter note = 144 bpm. Practice major and Lydian scales with both hands in four octaves, up and down the keyboard.

3. Practice major and Lydian scales with the right hand while comping syncopated major 7 chords in the left hand (see figure 1.3).

Fig. 1.3. Major/Lydian Scale Comping Exercise

THE LSTs AND USTs OF MAJOR 6/7

Using USTs will help you find harmonies for creating your interpretation of the tune. Let's explore the procedure for finding the triads associated with different chord/scale relationships.

We will organize these triads into two groups:

*   **LSTs** (lower-structure triads) consist only of chord tones.

*   **USTs** (upper-structure triads) include one or more tensions.

Major (Ionian): CMaJ6/7(9)

To find the LSTs and USTs for a C major 7 chord using the major scale:

1. Write out the C major scale.

Fig. 1.4. C Major Scale

2. Build triads diatonically on each scale degree.

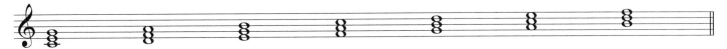

Fig. 1.5. C Major Scale Triads

3. Color in the notehead where each avoid note appears: scale degree 4.

Fig. 1.6. Triads with Avoid Notes in C Major

4. Label each scale degree's triad with a Roman numeral. Then analyze its chord quality. Below each Roman numeral, indicate whether the triad is an LST (no tensions) or UST (one or more tensions).

IMaj	II–	III–	IVMaj	VMaj	VI–	VII°
LST	UST	LST	UST	UST	LST	UST

Fig. 1.7. Major Scale: LSTs and USTs

5. Disqualify all triads which contain the avoid note.

Major 6/7 Triad Grid

The following "Triad Grid" for major 7 chords and the major scale will help you to organize which LSTs and USTs are associated with the tension-specific seventh chord.

Major 6/7 Chord: Major Scale

LSTs	USTs
I	VMaj7(9)
III– VI–	

Fig. 1.8. Major Scale Triad Grid

This grid shows that the LSTs for the major 6/7 chord are I major, III minor, and VI minor, built from its first, third, and sixth degrees. While LSTs do not contain tensions, they can be useful in harmonizing melodies and playing "inside" chord sound during improvisation.

The UST for major 6/7 is V major.

Roman Numeral Notation with LSTs and USTs

The Roman numerals in this book are used as an easily transposable numbering method, not as harmonic analysis. In the key of C major, an FMaj7(9) chord's UST V major would be C major, while the V of the key is G major. This book indicates the UST over the primary seventh chord separated by a horizontal line.

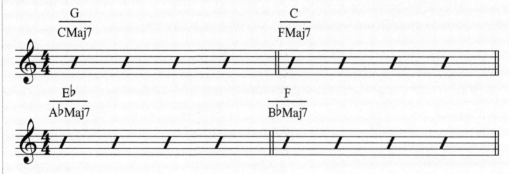

Fig. 1.9. UST's Based on Root of the Moment

Notation Note: In this book, LSTs and USTs are set above the primary chord symbol, separated by a horizontal line. This does not always imply full chord over chord. Often, the left-hand voicing is simply guide tones or guide tone + 1. In text, the UST and its related chord will be separated by a horizontal line, as in $\frac{G}{CMaj7}$ or by use of the word "over," as in G over CMaj7. A diagonal slash is used for hybrids and inversions: G/C or C/G.

UST V major is the most commonly used UST of the major 7 chord. For example, on C major 7, UST V major is a G major triad ($\frac{G}{CMaj7}$), just as on F major 7, UST V major is a C major triad ($\frac{C}{FMaj7}$).

LST VI minor contains scale degree 6 (13). Although it adds color, scale degree 6 is a chord tone thus VI minor is considered an LST. While both the 6 and 7 are in the major 7 family and can be used together as well as interchangeably, LST VI minor *cannot* be used over a major 7 in the LH. This is because VI minor contains the root of the primary chord, which clashes with the major 7th.

While II minor, IV major, and VII diminished are USTs, they contain the avoid note, scale degree 4 (11), which creates a ♭9 between the 3 and tension 11. Therefore, these triads are not used, and are called "unavailable." However, they can be used as passing chords in melodic harmonization.

Lydian

In Lydian, the replacement of 4 with ♯4 is a very important distinction. In Lydian, there are *no avoid notes*. All tensions in Lydian are available: 9, ♯11, 13.

By following the procedure shown for Ionian, we can arrive at these triads for Lydian, illustrated in figure 1.10 on CMaj7(9,♯11,13):

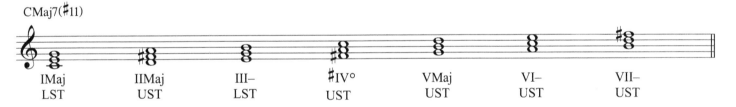

Fig. 1.10. C Lydian LSTs and USTs

Lydian Triad Grid

Maj6/7 Chord: Lydian

LSTs	USTs
I	IIMaj(9,♯11,13)
III–	♯IV°(♯11,13)
VI–	V(9)
	VII–(9,♯11)

Fig. 1.11. Lydian Triad Grid

The characteristic UST sound for Lydian is II major. VII minor is also often used. For example, UST II major on a C major 7 (9,♯11,13) chord is the D major triad. UST VII minor on C major 7 (9,♯11) is a B minor triad.

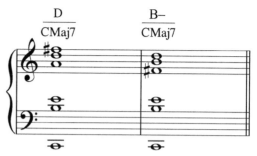

Fig. 1.12. Lydian USTs

The ♯IV° is used less because the tritone can sound like an unwanted D7 chord.

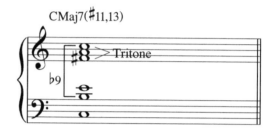

Fig. 1.13. ♯IV Diminished

The Lydian scale is not truly a substitute for the major scale just because the I chords are both major. The ♯11 should be handled with care and not overused, as it is a very unique sound. The Lydian and Ionian USTs both contain V major and VI minor, so use the ♯11 in your Lydian voicings to make the distinction between Lydian and Ionian.

IDENTIFYING USTS FROM CHORD SYMBOLS: TENSION CHART

The USTs you choose should be based on the tension specified in the chord symbol. When a chord symbol states Maj7(9,♯11), the UST must be VII minor. Similarly, when the chord symbol states Maj7(9), the UST is V major.

This chart summarizes the USTs for CMaj7 and FMaj7:

Indicated Tensions	UST	CMaj7	FMaj7
9	V	G / CMaj7	C / FMaj7
6	VI–	A– / CMaj6	D– / FMaj6
9, ♯11, 13	II	D / CMaj7	G / FMaj7
9, ♯11	VII–	B– / CMaj7	E– / FMaj7

Fig. 1.14. USTs based on Indicated Tensions

LEARNING USTs

Learning to name tension-specific USTs quickly is the first step in being able to comp chords quickly in tempo. A solid knowledge of scale degrees is important for quickly determining the USTs. Every time you encounter a major 7 chord, place a horizontal line above the chord and fill in the tension-specific UST by letter name (not Roman numeral). When no tensions are listed, use UST V major. Begin to associate all major 7 chords with USTs. Know and hear the sounds you are creating!

The following practice exercises will help you learn the sound of each major 7 UST and memorize which USTs go with which chords. Learn to memorize the major 7 Roman numerals for Ionian and Lydian and the tensions within each UST.

Strive for accuracy in reading specific tension combinations. Some jazz pianists think "the more tensions the better." A more thoughtful approach involves being selective about the particular sounds *you hear*.

Practice 1.2. Listening

Play a major 7 chord on the piano, and let it ring with the sustain pedal down. Strike the UST numerous times and really hear each tone against the chord quality (low register root, mid-register *guide tones*, discussed later this chapter). Then strike each note of the UST and sing the tension (or chord tone).

Fig. 1.15. Hearing Pitches of USTs: $\dfrac{G}{CMaj7}$

You may associate colors, moods, or a "dark" to "bright" spectrum to the notes as a way of recognizing the tensions. You may also notice that the tensions sound different above different chord qualities.

Practice 1.3. UST Recognition Practice for Major 7

For each chord in this chart, follow this procedure. Use figure 1.14 as a reference.

1. Identify the Roman numeral for the UST that contains the indicated tensions. For major 7 chords, the UST choices are V major, VI minor, II major, and VII minor, depending on the specified tensions. For example, if the given chord is D♭Maj7(9,♯11), you'd say VII minor.

2. Translate the Roman numeral into the letter name of the UST based on the root of the chord. For D♭Maj7(9,♯11), you'd write in C–.

3. Write the UST and a horizontal line above the chord symbol: $\dfrac{\text{C–}}{\text{D♭Maj(9,♯11)}}$.

1. $\underline{\beta}$ EMaj7(9)	2. GMaj7(9,♯11)	3. DMaj7(9,♯11,13)	4. A♭Maj7(9,♯11)
5. FMaj7(9)	6. B♭Maj7(9,♯11,13)	7. D♭Maj6	8. AMaj7(9,♯11,13)
9. G♭Maj7(9,♯11)	10. BMaj7(9,♯11)	11. FMaj6	12. C♭Maj7(9)
13. DMaj7(9)	14. GMaj7(9,♯11,13)	15. B♭Maj7(9,♯11)	16. F♯Maj7(9,♯11)
17. AMaj7(9)	18. DMaj6	19. E♭Maj7(9)	20. CMaj7(9,♯11)

CMaj7 UST VOICINGS

The pianist's role in most jazz and popular music is to supply the song's harmony and rhythm by playing the chords (comping). "Comping" is short for "accompanying." The purpose of this book is to teach you how to comp using USTs. In this section, we will learn to comp open-position voicings (larger than an octave) without the root (scale degree 1).

These voicings are used in group playing when there is a bass player (who plays the roots of the chords.)

Guide Tones in LH

The first set of voicings include the chord sound in the LH: guide tones 3 and 7. The RH plays the UST. Begin by familiarizing yourself with the guide tones of the major 7 chord: major 3rd and major 7th. For CMaj7, the 3rd is E and the 7th is B.

Either note can be on the top or bottom. If E is on the bottom, it is in first inversion; if B is on the bottom, it is in third inversion. Learn to play these guide tones with ease in both inversions.

You may sustain a low C to hear the guide tones in context as a CMaj7 chord.

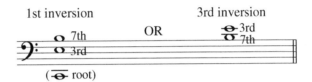

Fig. 1.16. Major 7 Guide Tones

Invert the guide tones and choose their octave to best support the rest of the voicing, avoiding low interval limits. The best range for these voicings is from D below middle C to A above middle C.

Practice 1.4. Guide Tones in First and Third Inversions

Practice guide tones in first and third inversions.

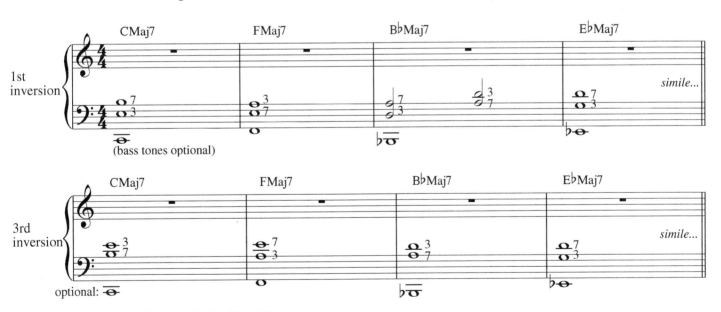

Fig. 1.17. Major 7 Guide Tone Practice

Tension Substitution (Guide Tones + 1)

Once the guide tones are familiar, add tension 9 to first inversion, and add the 5 to third inversion (guide tone + 1). The 13 may also be used, replacing the 5 in third inversion. When these chord tones are replaced by tensions, it is called "tension substitution."

The rule of tension substitution is: **Replace the root with the 9 and the 5 with the 13**. (These voicings only use T9.)

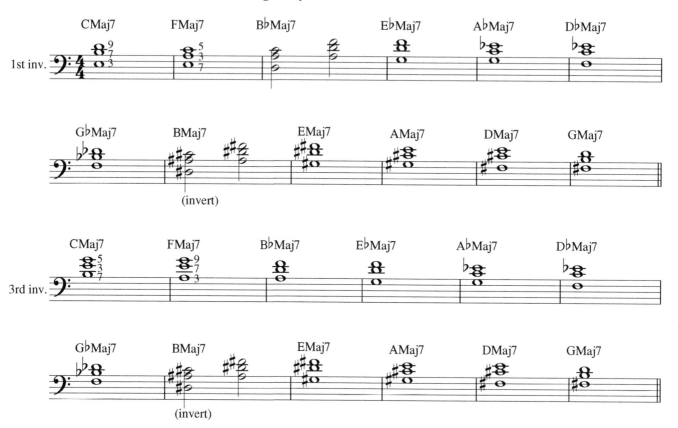

Fig. 1.18. Tension Substitutions in First and Third Inversions

Quartal Voicings in LH

As an alternative to the 3 and 7 in the LH, you can also play fourths: either 3, 6, 9 or 7, 3, 13. This gives more tension in the LH voicing, and the foundation of the voicing has the unique sound of fourths.

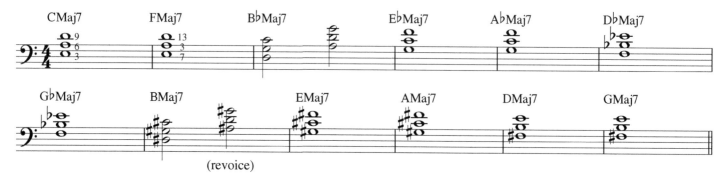

Fig. 1.19. LH Voicings in Fourths

Major 6 Voicing

For a major 6 voicing, you can place UST VI minor above fourths in the LH (3, 6, 9). When using VI minor in the RH, do not use the 7th degree of the chord In the LH because it creates a ♭9 between the major 7th of the chord and the third of VI minor UST (which is the root of the chord). Use V major in the RH to add scale degree 7 as an extra color above the 3, 6, 9 in the LH. This way, the voicing has 6, 7, and 9.

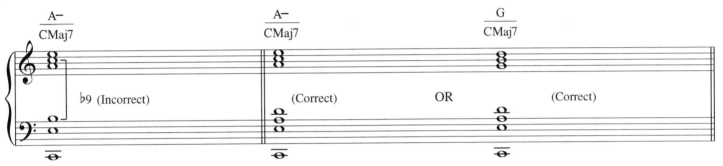

Fig. 1.20. Voicing CMaj7 and CMaj6

It is very important that you become confident with the LH voicings in both inversions. The LH builds the foundation for the open-position voicings. These LH voicings can also be used underneath the melody or improvisation in the RH. You can also play these voicings in your RH and add bass activity in your LH. Three great uses for one voicing!

USTs in RH

Next, add a UST in the RH above the chord sound in the LH. The USTs can be played:

- in any inversion
- from mid to high register
- with octave doubling of bottom note

For small voicings, play the guide tones in the LH and the UST in the RH in close proximity. As the register of the UST rises, add octave doublings in the RH, and support the higher top half of the voicing with a three-note mid-register voicing.

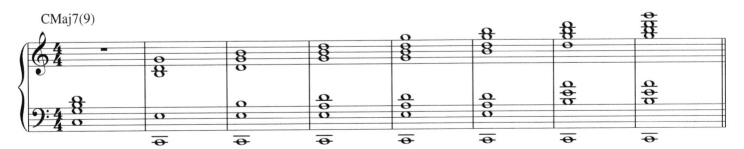

Fig. 1.21. Range and LH

Figure 1.22 voice leads the major 7 chord through the circle of fifths using fourths in the LH and UST V major with octave doubling in the RH. Continue to analyze the LH voicings.

Fig. 1.22. Open Position Major 7 Chords

Be Mindful of the "Chord of the Moment"

Avoid "rote" or hand-position memory without connecting to the chord of the moment. Always be aware of the chord you are playing without getting confused by the root of the UST versus the root of the chord being played.

Practice 1.5. Voicing Practice

Write out the voicings for the VI minor, II major, and VII minor USTs using this process:

1. Mark off four measures per line, and write in the major 7 chord symbol throughout the circle of fifths.

2. Write in horizontal lines over each chord, and then the letter name of the UST over that line.

3. Write out and voice lead USTs in the RH.

4. Use guide tones, guide tones + 1, or fourths in the LH (fourths for VI minor).

5. Play each voicing in all inversions out of tempo. *Really hear* the sounds you are creating, and work out numerous possibilities. Then, comp the chords in different keys, in tempo.

    Practice, memorize, experiment!

Practice 1.6. Comping Practice with Roots

Practice figure 1.23 using the following procedure as written, and then through the circle of fifths.

1. Play the root in the low register with the LH, unaccompanied.

2. Stride up, and play a 2- or 3-note LH voicing together with the UST in the RH.

3. Always voice lead the UST.

This way, you practice LH stride, LH voicings, and open-position UST voicing textures all at once!

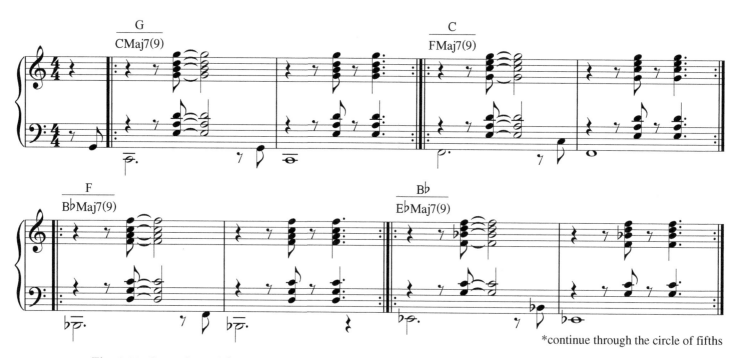

*continue through the circle of fifths

Fig. 1.23. Comping with Roots

Practice 1.7. Major 7 Workout

The "Major 7 Workout" on track 2 is a play along intended to help you exercise your LH and open-position voicings. Loop the recording for longer practice times.

1. Begin by practicing guide tones in each inversion (see figure 1.17). Practice until you can play with ease.

2. Play the guide tone + 1 voicing, and then the LH voicings in fourths (see figures 1.18 and 1.19).

3. When you feel confident in the LH voicings, choose a UST to play in your RH. Start simply: use V major UST in root position (see figure 1.21). Voice lead the USTs. Create a varied line with the top note of your voicings.

4. Play the "Major 7 Workout" in tempo through the circle of fifths. The harmonic rhythm is two measures per chord.

You can use track 2 to practice major 7 chords with USTs V major, VI minor, II major, and VII minor.

Major 7 Workout

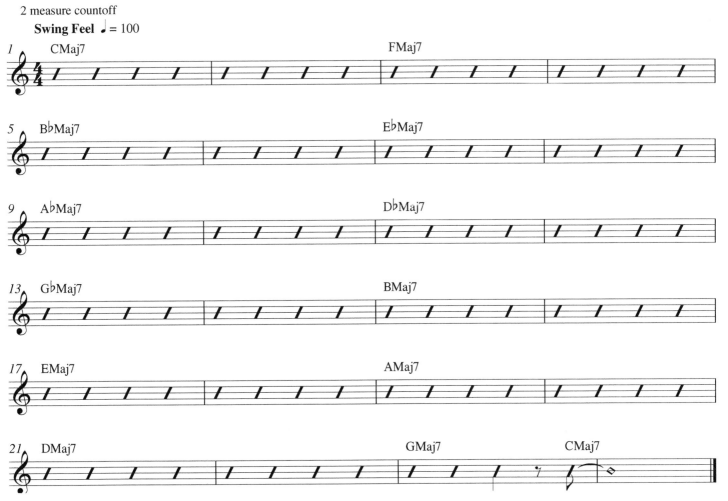

Fig. 1.24. Major 7 Workout

Practice 1.8. "Inner Courage"

3
with piano

4
without piano

Use the following approach to practice the tune "Inner Courage."

1. Listen to the comping example on track 3. Notice the approach to playing the voicings in terms of rhythmic interpretation, phrasing, and articulation under the melody and solo.

2. Play each chord as notated, one at a time, out of time, in order to really hear the voicing. For practice purposes, add the root in the lower register to anchor the sound.

3. Play through the chord sheet in tempo, using a fixed rhythm, along with track 4. This will help you to move the chord at the right time. The most important part is to move the chord right at the moment the chord symbol changes. Make the changes!

4. Improvise different inversions and rhythms with the chords during longer harmonic durations.

5. Refer to the "Inner Courage" Chord Sheet on page 18 for voicing examples.

"Inner Courage" Lead Sheet

2 measure countoff
Intro: Drums 4 bars

Suzanna Sifter

Form: 2 measure countoff
    Drum Intro: 4 bars
    Head
    1 chorus sax solo
    1 chorus piano solo
    Head out to Coda

Fig. 1.25. "Inner Courage" Lead Sheet

"Inner Courage" Chord Sheet

2 measure countoff
Intro: Drums 4 Bars

Suzanna Sifter

Medium Fast Swing ♩ = 104

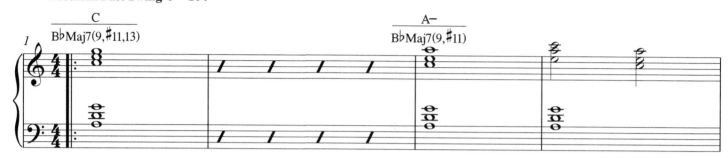

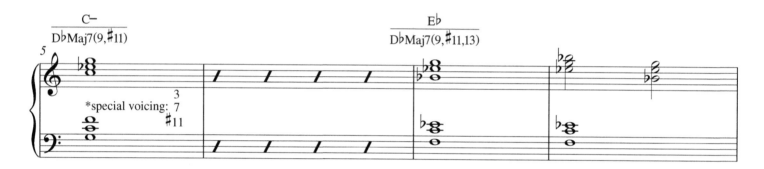

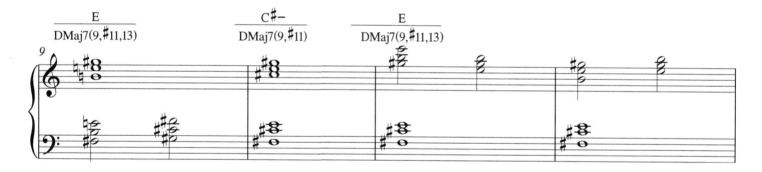

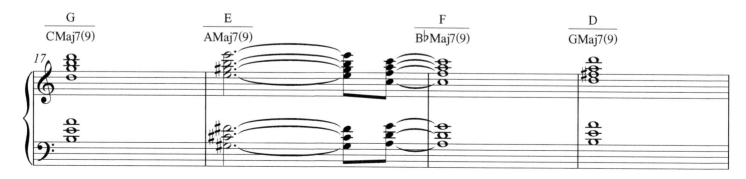

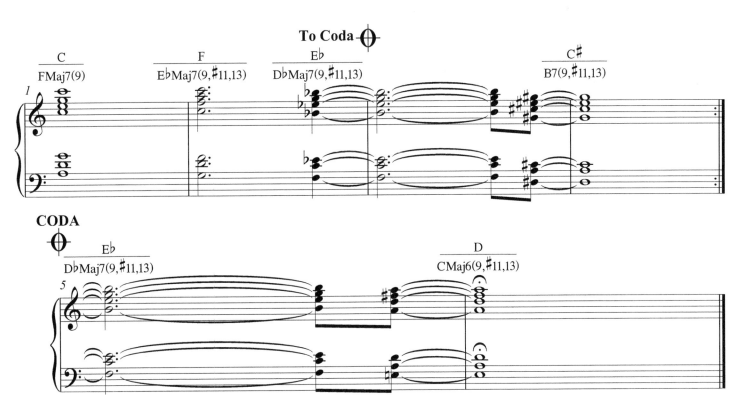

Fig. 1.26. "Inner Courage" Chords

Theory must be put into practice in real musical situations as soon as possible! Apply this knowledge by playing all major 7 chords with one of the UST formulas: V major, VI minor, II major, or VII minor. Make this a habit as you practice real tunes.

Try to memorize these new voicings as soon as possible. Do not rely on the written chord symbols past the point of working out the voicings and voice leading. Remember that the goal is to be able to interpret chord symbols on a lead sheet, with only the USTs written in. Eventually, you will be able to sight-read great sounding chords. Onward!

Dominant 7

In chapter 2, we will study dominant 7 chords and introduce the concept of "coupling triads." Jazz standards that include many dominant 7 chords are the blues, "Isotope," "I'm Walkin," "Freddie the Freeloader," and "Passion Dance" (dominant 7sus4).

CHORD SCALE

The chord scale of the dominant 7 chord is Mixolydian, the fifth mode of the major scale. Mixolydian is structured as a major scale with a flat 7. Thus, its I chord is a dominant 7: 1, 3, 5, ♭7.

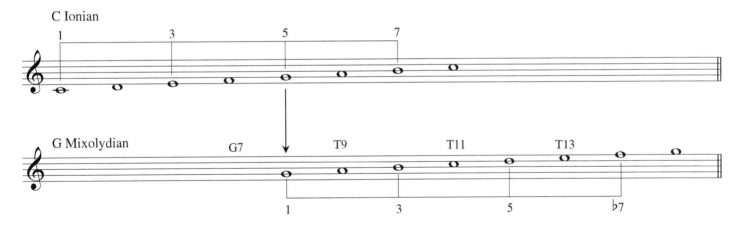

Fig. 2.1. Major Scale and Mixolydian Mode

7sus4

The I chord can also be a 7sus4: 1, 4, 5, ♭7. The 4th scale degree is "suspended" over the 3rd. In this case, the avoid note *is* the characteristic tone of the dominant 7sus4 chord.

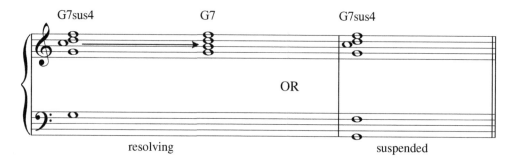

Fig. 2.2. Dominant 7sus4 Chord: Resolving or Suspended

Practice 2.1. Learning Dominant 7 Chords and the Mixolydian Mode

1. Practice all dominant 7 chords in all inversions.

2. Set the metronome to quarter note = 144 bpm. Practice all Mixolydian modes as quarter notes with both hands in four octaves, up and down the keyboard.

3. Practice all Mixolydian modes with the right hand while comping syncopated dominant 7 chords in the left hand.

Fig. 2.3. Mixolydian Mode Comping Exercise

*Note: You can practice the same scale with a 7sus4 chord in the LH.

THE LSTS AND USTS OF DOMINANT 7

This process will help you determine which triads are associated with dominant 7 chords.

Mixolydian: G7

1. Write out the G Mixolydian mode.

Fig. 2.4. G Mixolydian Mode

2. Build triads diatonically on each scale degree.

Fig. 2.5. G Mixolydian Triads

3. Color in the avoid note C, scale degree 4.

Fig. 2.6. G Mixolydian Triads/Avoid Note: C

4. Label each scale degree with a Roman numeral. Then analyze the chord quality and whether the triad is an LST or a UST.

IMaj	II−	III°	IVMaj	V−	VI−	♭VIIMaj
LST	UST	LST	UST	UST	UST	UST

Fig. 2.7. G Mixolydian Triads: LSTs and USTs

5. For dominant 7, you will disqualify all triads which contain scale degree 4.

Dominant 7 Triad Grid

The following grid shows the LSTs and USTs associated with dominant 7 chords and the Mixolydian mode.

Dominant 7 Chord: Mixolydian Mode

LSTs	USTs
I	V–(9)
III°	VI–(13)

Fig. 2.8. Dominant 7/Mixolydian Triad Grid

The LSTs for the dominant 7 chord are I major and III diminished built from its first and third degrees.

The most valuable USTs of dominant 7 using the Mixolydian mode are V minor and VI minor. V minor contains tension 9, and VI minor contains tension 13. For example, on G7(9), UST V minor is D–. On G7(13), UST VI minor is E–. These voicings can be written with the UST written above the primary chord, separated by a horizontal line. D– over G7(9) and E– over G7(13).

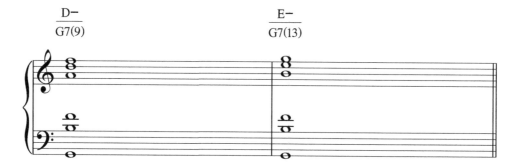

Fig. 2.9. Mixolydian Voicings with Tensions

Dominant 7sus4/Mixolydian

This grid shows the triads associated with dominant 7sus4 chords and the Mixolydian mode.

Dominant 7sus4: Mixolydian

LSTs	USTs
Isus4	II–(9,11,13)
	IV(11,13)
	♭VII(9,11)

Fig. 2.10. Dominant 7sus4 Formula Grid

USTs II minor, IV major, and ♭VII major all contain the avoid note on a dominant 7 chord, thus they are unavailable. However, these USTs work well on a dominant 7sus4 *because* they contain scale degree 4. The suspended 4 is considered a chord tone in a dominant 7sus4 chord.

Special Circumstance: Tension 10 on a 7sus4

The I major and VI minor chords (also III diminished) are considered USTs with the 3rd degree as tension 10 above the suspended 4th degree. Tension 10 is usually used during long harmonic duration of a suspended chord in a vamp or a tune such as McCoy Tyner's "Passion Dance."

The ♭VII major and II minor emphasize the dominant 7sus4 sound. For example, on G7sus4, the UST ♭VII major is an F triad, and UST II minor is an A minor triad. You can also extend the F triad to become an upper-structure 7 chord,

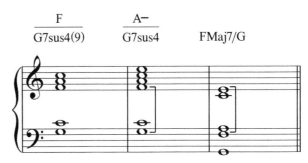

Fig. 2.11. G7sus4

adding the 13 to the UST with only the root in the LH (hybrid chord). These are common and effective ways of playing a dominant 7sus4 chord.

Tension Chart

When the chord symbol states dominant 7(13), the UST is VI minor. Similarly, when the chord symbol states dominant 7(9), the UST is V minor. This chart summarizes the most commonly used USTs for the F and C dominant 7 and dominant 7sus4 chords.

Indicated Tensions	UST	C7 and C7sus4	F7 and F7sus4
9	V–	G–/C7	C–/F7
13	VI–	A–/C7	D–/F7
9, 11, 13	II–	D–/C7sus4	G–/F7sus4
11, 13	IV	F/C7sus4	B♭/F7sus4
9, 11	♭VII	B♭/C7sus4	E♭/F7sus4
10, 13	VI–	A–/C7sus4	D–/F7sus4

Practice 2.2. UST Recognition Practice for Dominant 7

Write in the tension specific UST(s) for each given chord.

1. $\dfrac{\text{E-}}{\text{A7(9)}}$	2. F#7(9,13)	3. D♭7sus4(9,11)	4. E7sus4(9,11,13)
5. A♭7sus4(9,11)	6. F7(9,13)	7. C7(9)	8. B♭7(13)
9. D♭7sus4(10,13)	10. E7(9)	11. B7sus4(9,11,13)	12. F7(13)
13. C#7sus4(9,11)	14. E♭7(9,13)	15. G7(9)	16. D7sus4(10, 13)
17. G♭7(9,13)	18. C7sus4(9,11,13)	19. A♭7(9)	20. E♭7sus4(9,11)

DOMINANT 7 UST VOICINGS

Practice 2.3. Guide Tones in LH

The guide tones for dominant 7 chords are 3 and ♭7. In the case of G7, the 3 is B and the ♭7 is F. Practice the guide tones for dominant 7 chords in both inversions, throughout the circle of fifths.

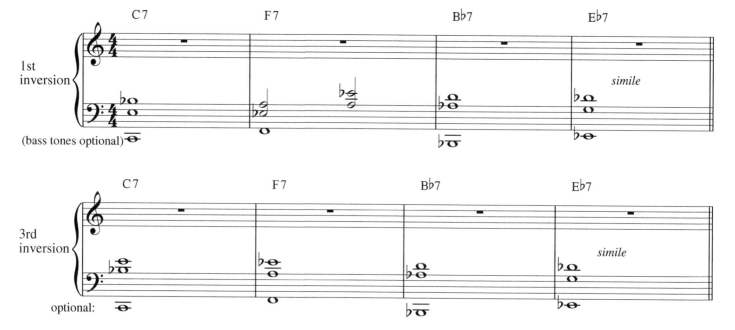

Fig. 2.12. Dominant 7 Guide-Tones Practice

These guide tones are intended for the LH range. Note that the guide tones cycle back to the same voicings in both inversions.

Practice Tips: LH Guide Tones

- Notice how each note slides down a half step through the progression.

- Do not play by rote. Always connect the guide tones to the chord.

- Stride up from the root, and play the guide tones with your LH in tempo.

- Memorize the guide tones without writing them down.

Remember, the final goal is interpreting chord symbols, not reading voicings. Apply your new knowledge to the piano as soon as possible!

GUIDE TONES + 1

Once the guide tones are familiar, add tension 9 in first inversion, and add tension 13 in third inversion. Tension 9 takes the place of the root, and tension 13 takes the place of the 5.

Practice 2.4. Guide Tone + 1 in LH

Play these voicings through the circle of fifths twice, beginning in both first and third inversions.

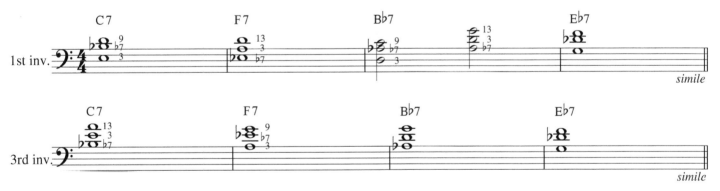

Fig. 2.13. Guide Tone + 1

You can invert the chord, rather than octave jump, any time the chord is getting too low or too high (see figure 2.13, measure 3). However, *always voice lead at the point of chord change!*

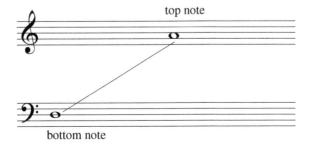

Fig. 2.14. LH Voicing Range

Practice 2.5. Adding USTs to LH Voicings

Next, add either UST V minor
(T9) or VI minor (T13) in the
RH above the chord sound in
the LH.

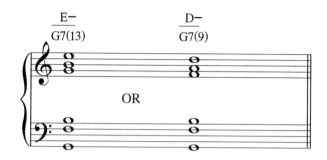

Fig. 2.15. Lydian USTs

Be aware that when using
the V minor UST in the RH and
♭7, 3, 13 in the LH, a ♭9 is created
between the ♭7(B♭) above the 13
(A) in the LH. When you don't
want this sound, either invert
the UST or play the 5 instead of
the 13 in the LH.

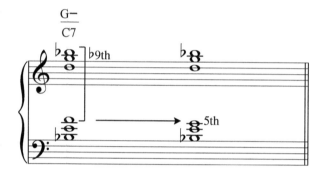

Fig. 2.16. Lydian USTs

Practice 2.6. Voice Leading through Circle of Fifths

Practice voice leading the dominant 7 chord through the circle of fifths, using
3-note voicings in the LH and USTs V minor and VI minor in the RH. Continue
to analyze the LH voicings.

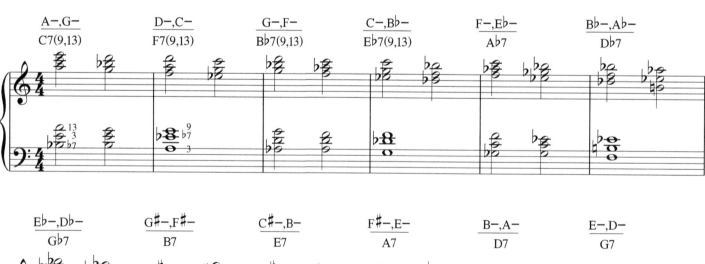

Fig. 2.17. Dominant 7 Open-Position Voicings

Practice voice leading the dominant 7sus4 chord through the circle of fifths, using fourths in the LH (1, 4, 7 or 5, 1, 4) and UST II minor in the RH.

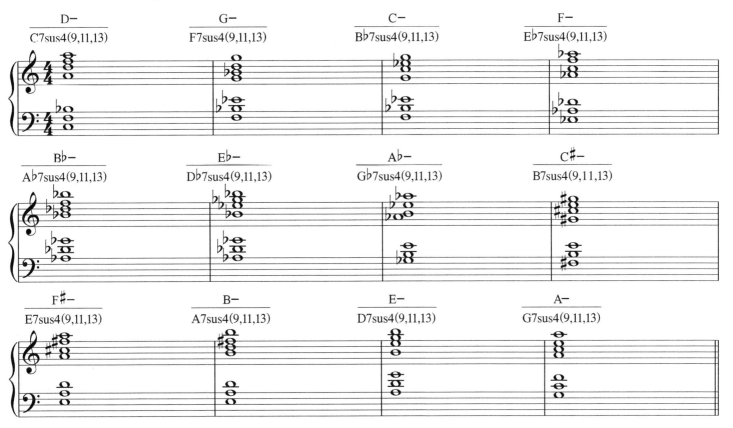

Fig. 2.18. Dominant 7sus4 Open Position Voicings

The USTs can be played in any inversion, with and without octave doublings of the bottom note. Practice each chord as a vamp, improvising the same chord in a multitude of inversions and rhythms in tempo. Begin with V minor, and then practice VI minor. Then apply it to a progression. Work the same process for the C7sus4 chord using USTs II minor and ♭VII major with scale degrees 1, 4, 7 in the LH.

COUPLING TRIADS

Coupling triads are two triads a step apart used to add tension and motion to a chord. In figure 2.19, both USTs of G7 are played in succession as coupling triads, one after the other, changing inversions. In this case, the use of both triads expresses both T9 and T13.

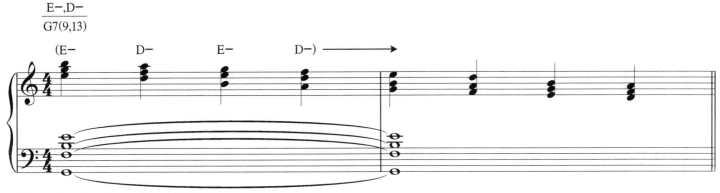

* Bass plays low G or stride with LH

Fig. 2.19. Mixolydian Coupling Triads

Coupling triads can be used to add harmonic motion for the duration of a chord. You can also add chromatic motion between the VI minor and V minor.

*Bass plays low G or stride with L.H.

Fig. 2.20. Coupling Triads with Chromatic Motion

Practice 2.7. Comping Practice with Roots

Practice each dominant 7 unaccompanied in tempo, striding down to the root, four measures per key. Continue throughout the circle of fifths.

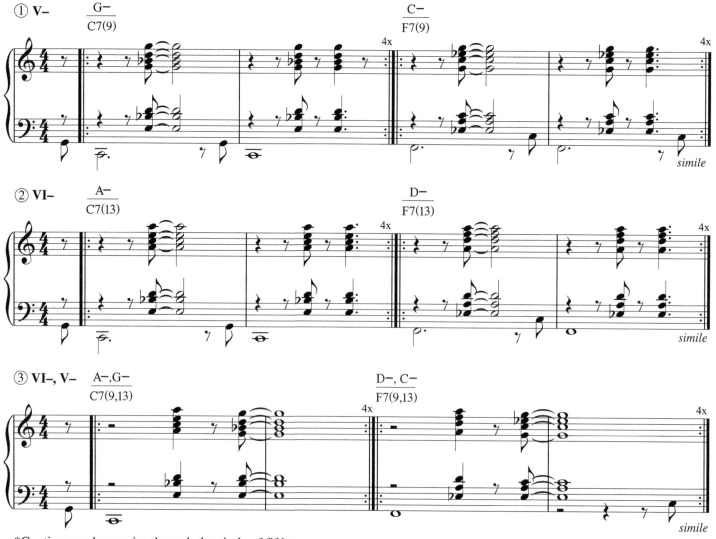

*Continue each exercise through the circle of fifths.

Fig. 2.21. UST V Minor and VI Minor Comping Practice with Roots

Practice 2.8. Dominant 7 in Twelve Keys

Track 5 takes you through the dominant chords in the circle of fifths.

First, practice the guide tones and then guide tone + 1 voicings separately in the LH. Next, play the entire dominant 7 chord with each UST in the RH. Begin with V minor, and then practice VI minor. Then play both USTs as coupling triads.

Dominant 7 Workout

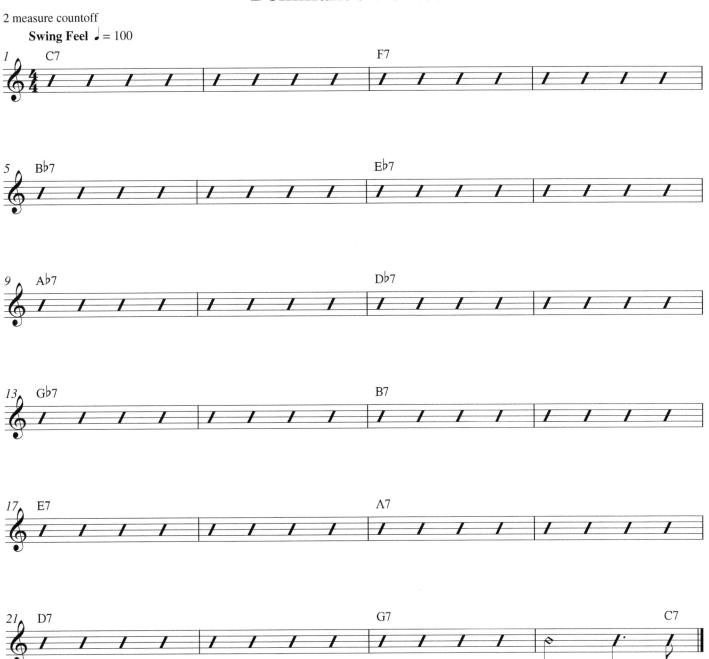

Fig. 2.22. Dominant 7 Workout

Practice 2.9. Combining V7 with I

V7 IMaj7 Workout

This workout combines dominant 7 with major 7 (chapter 1). It begins with the dominant chord for two measures, resolves to the major 7 chord for two measures, and then changes keys. Choose a tension, then write in the corresponding USTs above the seventh chords.

Improvise voicing inversions and comping rhythms throughout these V7 I progressions. Be aware of what chord you are playing; know the difference between the root of the UST verses the root of the 7 chord being played. Use your ears and rhythmic sense to add forward motion to the progression.

V7 IMaj7 Workout

Fig. 2.23. V7 IMaj7 Workout

Practice 2.10. Blues

Blues Workout

The "Blues Workout" takes you through two choruses in three keys: C, F, and Bb. Practice varied tensions and voicings in each chorus, culminating in three notes in the LH and four notes in the RH (octave doubling). The piano plays on first chorus only.

Blues Workout

Fig. 2.24. Standard Blues Progression

Practice Tips: Blues Progression

- Write in either or both USTs over each chord.
- Work out three different sets of voicings to enhance your comping vocabulary.
- Set varied voicings, from four to seven parts.
- Transpose the progression to F and B♭.
- Comp freely, and listen to the new sounds you are creating!

Practice 2.11. "Talkin'"

8
with piano

9
without piano

Practice "Talkin'" using the following approach.

1. Listen to the full band version on track 8, paying particular attention to how the piano comping fits in with the melody and interacts with the soloist. Refer to the "Talkin" chord sheet on page 36 for voicing examples. Note that the written voicings sometimes differ from the recorded voicings. The written voicings are a good place to start.

2. Play each chord out of tempo, one at a time, as notated, in order to really hear the voicing. Add the root in the lower register to anchor the sound.

3. Play through the lead sheet with track 9. Add your own rhythms and accompaniment to the melody and sax solo. You can improvise your own solo after the sax. Try using USTs as melodic material!

"Talkin'" Lead Sheet

Form: 1 measure countoff
     I measure drums
     Head
     Sax Solo 1 Chorus
     Pno Solo 1 Chorus
     D.S. al Coda

Fig. 2.25. "Talkin'" Lead Sheet

"Talkin'" Chord Sheet

Suzanna Sifter

Fig. 2.26. "Talkin'" Chords

Apply these concepts whenever you encounter dominant 7 chords in any tunes you play. Writing in the USTs over the written chords will help you build the habit of connecting the chord symbol to the UST. In the next chapter, we will look at minor 7 chords.

CHAPTER 3

Minor 7

In chapter 3, we look at the minor 7 chord, which like the dominant 7 is prominent in the major key II V I progression, so emblematic in jazz. Jazz standards for practicing minor 7 chords include minor blues tunes such as "Mr. PC" and "Stolen Moments" and tunes in minor keys such as "Beautiful Love" and "Sugar." Jazz standards good for modal practice are: "Impression," "So What," and "Footprints."

CHORD SCALE

The chord scale of the minor 7 chord in a II–7 V7 IMaj7 progression is Dorian. Dorian is the second mode of the major scale, structured as a major scale with a flat 3 and flat 7. The I chord in Dorian is a minor 7: 1, ♭3, 5, ♭7.

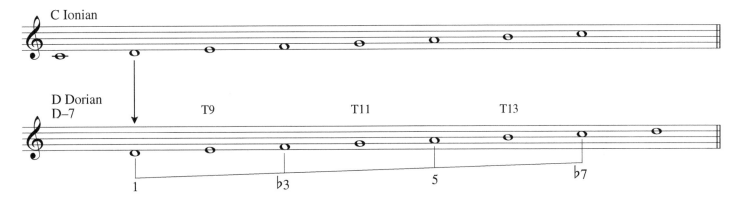

Fig. 3.1. Major Scale and Dorian Mode

There are many other chord scale options for the minor 7 chord, such as natural minor (Aeolian), harmonic minor, and melodic minor. Each scale has varied USTs. In this chapter, we will focus on Dorian.

Practice 3.1. Learning Minor 7 Chords and the Dorian Scale

1. Practice all minor 7 chords in all inversions.

2. Set the metronome to quarter note = 72 bpm on beats 2 and 4. Play the scales as swing eighth notes with both hands in four octaves, up and down the keyboard.

3. Practice scales with the right hand while comping syncopated minor 7 chords in the left hand (see figure 3.2).

Fig. 3.2. Dorian Mode Comping Exercise

THE LSTS AND USTS OF MINOR 7: D–7

To determine which triads are associated with minor 7 chords:

1. Write out the D Dorian mode.

Fig. 3.3. D Dorian Mode

2. Build triads diatonically on each degree.

Fig. 3.4. D Dorian Triads

3. Label each degree with a Roman numeral. Then analyze the chord quality and whether the triad is an LST or UST.

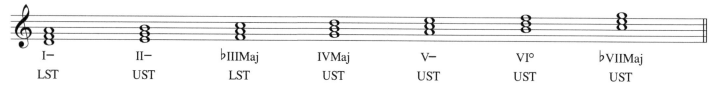

Fig. 3.5. D Dorian Triads: LSTs and USTs

Minor 7 Triad Grid

The following grid lists the LSTs and USTs associated with the minor 7 chord using the Dorian mode.

Minor 7 Chord: Dorian

LSTs	USTs
I– ♭III	II–(9,11,13) IV(11,13) V–(9) VI°(13) ♭VII(9,11)

Fig. 3.6. Dorian Triads

The LSTs for a minor 7 chord are I minor and ♭III major built from its first and flat third degrees.

The V minor and ♭VII major are the most commonly used USTs on minor 7 chords. V minor contains the 9 (like dominant 7), and ♭VII major contains 9 and 11. For instance, on a D–7 chord, UST V minor is an A minor triad, which contains tension 9; UST ♭VII major is a C major triad, which contains tensions 9 and 11.

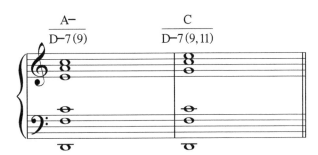

Fig. 3.7. Dorian Voicings with USTs

The UST II minor is most often used in modal settings or long harmonic durations. IV major works well as a coupling triad to V minor (or major). The tritone in VI diminished makes the chord sound more like a G7 than D–7; thus, it isn't used much harmonically.

Avoid using 13 on the II chord of a II V I progression. The 13 on the II chord is the third of the V chord, thus "giving away" the resolution of the guide tones of the II–7 V7. For example, in the key of C, the 7th of the D–7 chord (C) resolves to the 3rd of the G7 chord (B) to create the resolution of a II–7 V7 progression. When the B sounds on the D–7 chord early, it makes the II–7 sound like the V7 (G7).

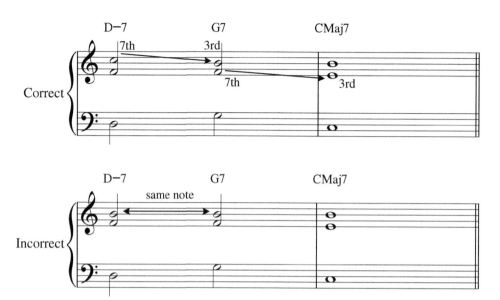

Fig. 3.8. Tension 13 Unavailable on II–7 Chord

Continue to use tension specific USTs. When the chord symbol states –7(9), the UST must be V minor. Similarly, when the chord symbol states –7(9,11), the UST is ♭VII major.

Tension Chart

To summarize, the UST formulas for a minor 7 chord using the Dorian scale on C–7 and F–7 are:

Indicated Tensions	UST	C–7	F–7
9	V–	$\dfrac{\text{G–}}{\text{C–7}}$	$\dfrac{\text{C–}}{\text{F–7}}$
9, 11	♭VII	$\dfrac{\text{B♭}}{\text{C–7}}$	$\dfrac{\text{E♭}}{\text{F–7}}$
11, 13	IV	$\dfrac{\text{F}}{\text{C–7}}$	$\dfrac{\text{B♭}}{\text{F–7}}$
9, 11, 13	II–	$\dfrac{\text{D–}}{\text{C–7}}$	$\dfrac{\text{G–}}{\text{F–7}}$

Memorize the Roman numerals for the Dorian chord scale. Continue to be aware of the tensions you are playing.

Use the same method to study the alternate chord scales such as Aeolian, harmonic minor, and melodic minor for varied tensions and tension combinations. For example, the minor 6 and minor (major 7) chords come from the melodic-minor scale and use USTs IV major and V major. Also, study the minor 7 chord as a "I– chord" (tonic minor) and "IV– chord" (subdominant minor).

Practice 3.2. UST Recognition Practice for Minor 7

Write in the associated UST for each given chord.

1. **D♯-**	2.	3.	4.
C♯–7(9, 11, 13)	F–7(9,11)	G♭–7(9)	B♭–7(9,11)
5.	6.	7.	8.
C–7(9)	E–7(9,11,13)	G♭–7(9,11,13)	E–7(9,11)
9.	10.	11.	12.
B–7(9)	A♭–7(9,11)	G–7(9,11,13)	D♭–7(9)
13.	14.	15.	16.
B–7(9,11,13)	E♭–7(9)	F♯–7(9,11)	A–7(9,11)
17.	18.	19.	20.
F–7(9,11,13)	B♭–7(9)	D–7(9,11)	A–7(9)

MINOR 7 UST VOICINGS

Practice 3.3. Guide Tones in LH

The guide tones of a minor 7 chord are the ♭3 and ♭7. In the case of D–7, the ♭3 is F and the ♭7 is C.

Practice the guide tones for the following minor 7 chords in both inversions, throughout the circle of fifths.

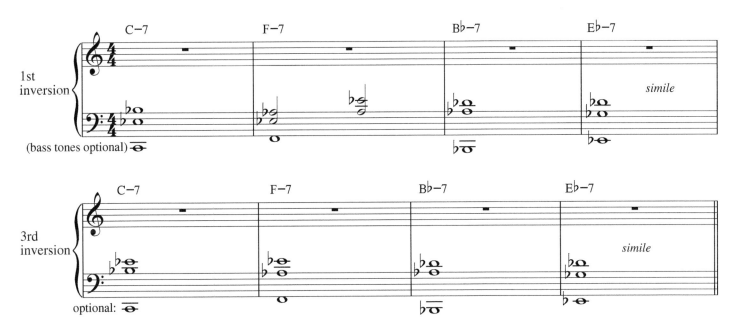

Fig. 3.9. Minor 7 Guide Tones Practice

Practice Tips:

- You may change inversions at any point *during* a chord.

- Always voice lead at the point of chord change.

- It helps to look ahead towards a target chord determined by range and work your way back through the voicings in order to avoid note range extremes (either too high or low).

Practice 3.4. Guide Tone + 1 in LH

Once the guide tones are familiar, add tension 9 to first inversion, and add the 5 to third inversion. (In tonal situations, the 13 is omitted.) Practice these voicings through the circle of fifths twice, beginning in both first and third inversions.

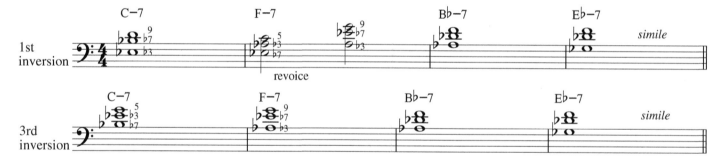

Fig. 3.10. Minor 7: Guide Tone + 1

Practice 3.5. Adding USTs to LH Voicings

Next, add either UST V minor (T9) or ♭VII major (T9,T11) in the RH above the chord sound in the LH.

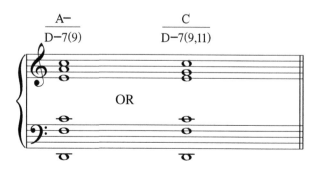

Fig. 3.11. UST V Minor or ♭VII Major over Minor 7

Practice 3.6. Open-Position Voice Leading

Practice voice leading the minor 7 chord through the circle of fifths using 3-note voicings in the LH and UST ♭VII major with octave doublings in the RH. You can use the same LH voicings to work on UST V minor. Subsequently, use any inversion, with and without octave doubling.

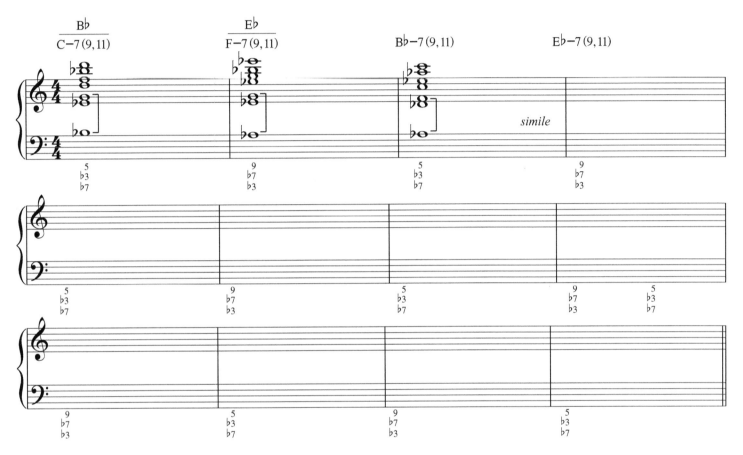

Fig. 3.12. Minor 7 Chords through the Circle of Fifths

You may use practice progressions other than the circle of fifths. Try moving the chords up or down in minor and major thirds, whole and half steps, and in augmented fourths. The following practice progressions can be used with any chord quality.

Progression 1

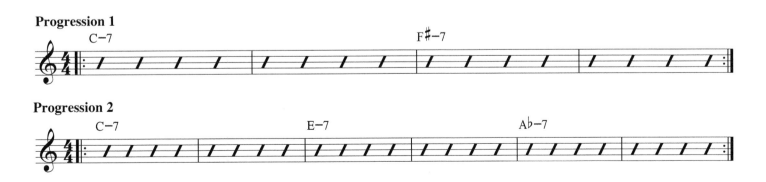

Progression 2

Progression 3

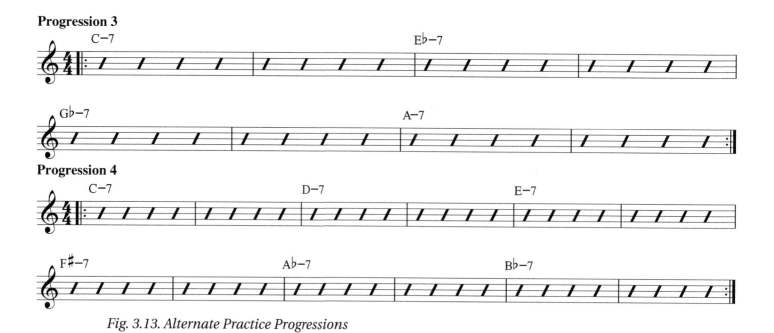

Fig. 3.13. Alternate Practice Progressions

Practice 3.7. Open-Position Comping

Minor 7 Workout

Choose one UST at a time, and use track 10 to practice your LH and open-position voicings in tempo. The *harmonic rhythm* (duration a chord lasts) is two measures per chord. Use one UST per chord throughout the progression, and then repeat the exercise with a different UST. You can also play coupling triads IV major and V minor, and even ♭VII major and I minor (even though I minor is an LST).

Minor 7 Workout

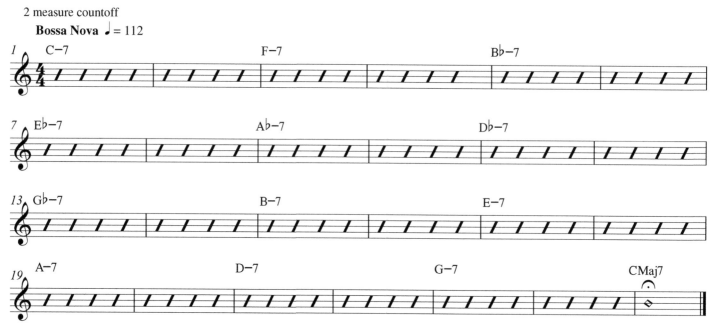

Fig. 3.14. Open Position Comping

TENSIONS 9, 13, AND MINOR 7

Minor 7 chords almost always take tension 9 and often an 11. Tension 13 is not used on a II–7 V7. When no specific tensions are named in the chord symbol, interpret the tensions in the chord progression based on your ear, your knowedge of jazz harmony, and the melody.

When working with a vocalist or instrumental soloist who plays the ♭3 in the melody, do not harmonize the ♭3 by playing a 9 at the top of your voicing. This creates a ♭9 (minor 2nd) between the ♭3 and the 9, which causes tuning problems. When playing solo or trio, the sound can be acceptable, if the voicing is balanced correctly. (Bill Evans did it!)

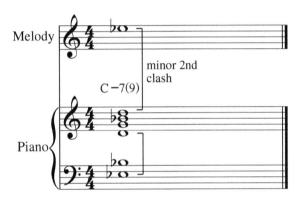

Fig. 3.15. Avoid –7(9) When ♭3 Is on Top

Practice 3.8. Combining II–7 with V7

11

II V Voicing Workout

Combine the minor 7 with dominant 7 (chapter 2) to form a II–7 V7 progression. This workout begins with the minor 7 chord for two measures, resolves to the dominant 7 down a fifth, then changes keys. You can vary the USTs you use on the dominant chord, but remember that since this progression is a II V, you can only use ♭VII major or V minor on the II–7 chord in the RH.

II V Voicing Workout

Fig. 3.16. II V Voicing Workout

It is very important to use your new voicings in real musical settings. Read through *The Real Book* placing a corresponding UST over every major, dominant, and minor 7 chord you find.

Practice 3.9. "Sorrow's End"

12
with piano

13
without piano

Practice "Sorrow's End" using the following approach.

1. Play the intro and interlude as written on the chord sheet, page 48.

2. Play through the lead sheet in tempo, playing the root and 5th on beat 1 and the full chord on beat 2.

3. When the chord is the same for two measures, use different inversions of voicings. At this point, the low register fifths are no longer necessary.

4. Listen to the interplay between all the instruments on track 12.

5. Listen to how *your own* accompaniment would fit in on track 13!

"Sorrow's End" Lead Sheet

As performed on the CD *Awakening* by Suzanna Sifter

Suzanna Sifter

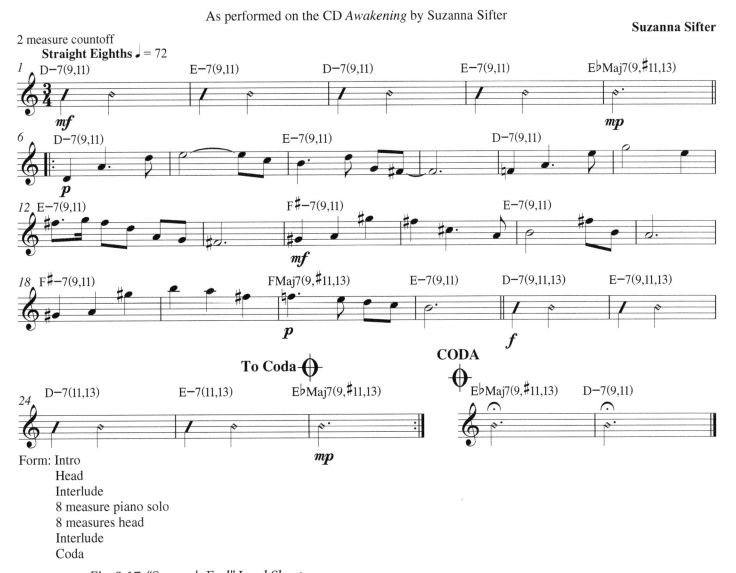

Form: Intro
    Head
    Interlude
    8 measure piano solo
    8 measures head
    Interlude
    Coda

Fig. 3.17. "Sorrow's End" Lead Sheet

"Sorrow's End" Chord Sheet

Suzanna Sifter

Fig. 3.18. "Sorrow's End" Chords

At this point, we have studied the major 7, dominant 7, and minor 7 chords, which are the harmonic content of the major II V I. Apply your new knowledge of USTs in all the tunes you play. Utilize your new USTs in tunes such as "Lady Bird," "Tune Up," and "Just Friends."

We will study the various possibilities of UST combinations within the context of the II V I later, in chapters 6 and 7. Next, in chapter 4, we will study the minor 7♭5.

Minor 7♭5

In chapter 4, we look at minor 7♭5 chords. Minor 7♭5 chords are often used as the II chord in the minor-key II V I progression. In minor, the II–7♭5 is used in partnership with a dominant 7 with altered tensions (♭9,♭13) and a minor I chord: II–7♭5 V7♭9 I–6. Suggested standards for practicing –7♭5 USTs are "Woody 'n' You," "Alone Together," and "Windows."

CHORD SCALE

When a pianist sees a minor 7♭5 chord, two scales come to mind: Locrian and Locrian natural 9. Locrian is the seventh mode of the major scale, and Locrian natural 9 is the sixth mode of the melodic-minor scale. (Another option is Locrian natural 9, natural 13, which is the second mode of the harmonic-major scale.)

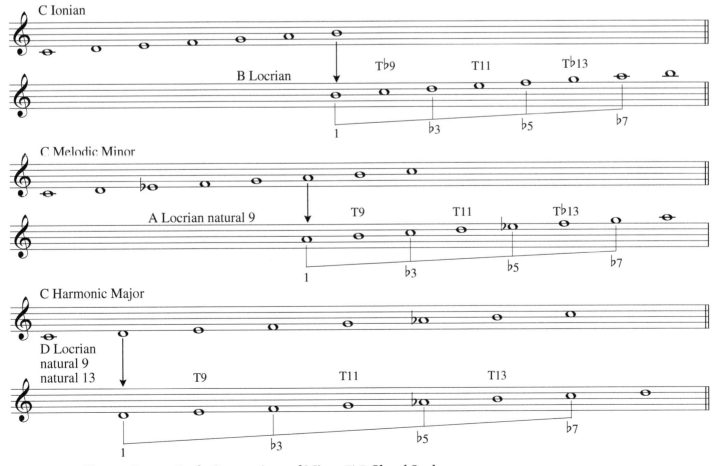

Fig. 4.1. Parent Scale Comparison of Minor 7♭5 Chord Scales

All of these scales have a minor 7♭5 as the I chord: 1 ♭3 ♭5 ♭7. Locrian natural 9 is a popular chord scale choice, because the natural 9 is a bright tension against the darker minor 7♭5 chord. This chapter will focus on Locrian natural 9 as the chord scale for the minor 7♭5 chord.

Practice 4.1. Learning Minor 7♭5 Chords and the Locrian Natural 9 Mode

Continue to use the practice methods from previous chapters to familiarize yourself with the minor 7♭5 chord in various inversions. Also play the Locrian natural 9 mode in the RH with LH syncopation of the minor 7♭5 chord in the LH.

Fig. 4.2. Locrian Natural 9 Mode Comping Exercise

THE LSTS AND USTS OF MINOR 7♭5: B–7♭5

To determine which triads are associated with minor 7♭5 chords using the Locrian natural 9 mode:

1. Write out the B Locrian natural 9 mode.

Fig. 4.3. B Locrian Natural 9 Mode

2. Build triads diatonically on each scale degree. (Note: There are two USTs on scale degrees 2 and ♭7.)

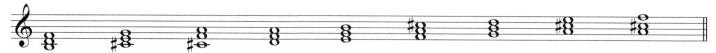

Fig. 4.4. B Locrian Natural 9 Triads

3. Label each scale degree with a Roman numeral. Then analyze the chord quality, and state whether the triad is an LST or UST.

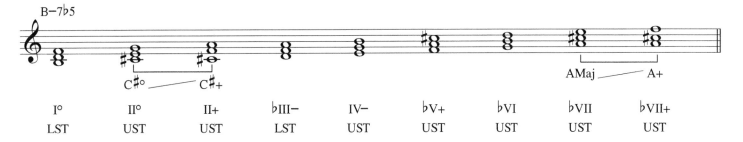

Fig. 4.5. B Locrian Natural 9 Triads: LSTs and USTs

Minor 7♭5 Triad Grid

The following grid lists the LSTs and USTs associated with the minor 7♭5 chord using the Locrian natural 9 mode.

Minor 7♭5 Chord: Locrian Natural 9

LSTs	USTs	
I°	II°(9,11,♭13)	♭VI(♭13)
♭III–	II+(9)	♭VII(9,11)
	IV–(11,♭13)	♭VII+(9)
	♭V+(9)	

Fig. 4.6. Minor 7♭5 Locrian Natural 9 Triads

The LSTs for the minor 7♭5 chord, using the 1 and ♭3 of the Locrian natural 9 mode, are I diminished and ♭III minor, built from degrees 1 and ♭3 of Locrian natural 9.

The most frequently used USTs are II augmented and ♭VII major because they contain tensions 9 and 9,11. The II augmented, ♭VII augmented, and ♭V augmented are all the same triad; thus, simply memorize II augmented and invert the triad for different voicings. When using parent scales other than the modes of the major scale, check to see if any chord tone has multiple USTs based from it. In this case, there are two possible USTs from scale degrees 2 and ♭7.

Fig. 4.7. More than One UST Quality on Same Scale Degree

Also be aware of the enharmonics: scale degree ♭5 in UST II augmented written as an E♯ can also be seen as an F in UST ♭V augmented.

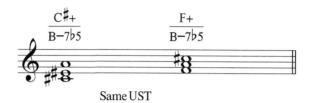

Fig. 4.8. Enharmonics

Flat 13 is a dissonant sound on the unstable minor 7♭5 chord, so it is usually used in progressions where the minor 7♭5 chord is of long harmonic duration. When the harmonic duration is shorter, as usual with a minor II V, use USTs II augmented and ♭VII rather than II diminished, IV minor, or ♭VI.

Tension Chart

To summarize, the most common UST formulas for a minor 7♭5 chord using the Locrian natural 9 scale on C–7♭5 and F–7♭5 are:

Indicated Tensions	UST	C–7♭5	F–7♭5
9	II+ (♭V+,♭VII+)	$\dfrac{\text{D+}}{\text{C–7♭5}}$	$\dfrac{\text{G+}}{\text{F–7♭5}}$
9, 11	♭VII	$\dfrac{\text{B♭}}{\text{C–7♭5}}$	$\dfrac{\text{E♭}}{\text{F–7♭5}}$

Practice 4.2. UST Recognition Practice for Minor 7♭5

Write in the associated UST for each given chord.

1. E–7♭5(9,11)	2. A♭–7♭5(9,11)	3. D♭–7♭5(9)	4. A–7♭5(9)
5. D♭–7♭5(9,11)	6. C♯–7♭5(9)	7. D–7♭5(9,11)	8. E♭–7♭5(9)
9. F♯–7♭5(9,11)	10. G–7♭5(9)	11. B♭–7♭5(9,11)	12. G♭–7♭5(9)
13. B–7♭5(9)	14. F♯–7♭5(9,11)	15. D–7♭5(9)	16. C–7♭5(9,11)
17. G–7♭5(9)	18. B–7♭5(9,11)	19. F–7♭5(9,11)	20. A♭–7♭5(9)

MINOR 7♭5 VOICINGS

The guide tones for the minor 7♭5 chord are ♭3 and ♭7. Usually, the ♭5 must also appear in the LH as an additional guide tone, because it is an altered chord tone and the characteristic note. If the ♭5 chord tone is in the RH voicing, such as in UST II augmented, the usual ♭3 and ♭7 will work. When playing UST ♭VII major, the LH needs to contain the ♭5; otherwise, it will sound like a minor chord.

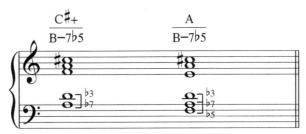

Fig. 4.9. Guide Tones ♭3 and ♭7 and ♭3, ♭5, ♭7

Practice 4.3. Minor 7♭5 LH Voicings

Practice the I diminished LST in your LH in all inversions throughout the circle of fifths. These LH voicings are applicable to both minor 7♭5 and diminished 7 chords. Complete the LH voicings in figure 4.10. Use the inversion written underneath each chord to guide your voice leading.

Fig. 4.10. LH Worksheet: Minor 7♭5 with LST I Diminished

Practice 4.4. Adding USTs to LH Voicings

Next, add UST ♭VII major with the RH to LST I diminished in the LH. The UST adds tensions 9 and 11 to the voicing. The root in the LH can be used in the lower mid register in the LH voicing (any inversion) because it gives the chord more stability. When you only want to use tension 9, use UST II augmented. Because this triad contains ♭5, you can omit the ♭5 from your LH, and just keep ♭3 and ♭7.

The presence of either the ♭7 or °7 is *very important*: it distinguishes the minor 7♭5 from the diminished 7 chord!

Practice 4.5. Open-Position Voice Leading

Complete the open-position voicings in figure 4.11 using UST ♭VII major. You can also practice UST II augmented, with ♭3 and ♭7 in the LH. Work with different inversions of the USTs.

1. Write in chord symbols through the circle of fifths.

2. Write in USTs over the chord symbols.

3. Write out the LH voicings.

4. Write out the USTs, using voice leading.

5. Practice, memorize, experiment!

Fig. 4.11. Minor 7♭5 Chords through the Circle of Fifths. Note that these voicings are true polychords due to the full triad in the LH.

Playing the USTs melodically will develop your ability to hear the 9 and 11 against a minor 7♭5 chord. These same tensions sound different in varied chord qualities, such as minor or diminished. Play each chord slowly, and really hear beyond the dissonance of the chord in order to get to know the sound, especially to distinguish it from the diminished 7 chord.

Practice 4.6. Comping Practice with Roots

Also practice these voicings solo through the circle of fifths, in tempo, eight measures per key. Work on striding down to the roots and striking these large spread voicings in concert.

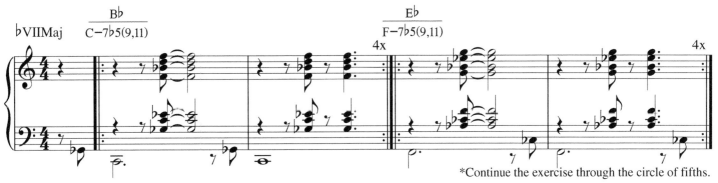

*Continue the exercise through the circle of fifths.

Fig. 4.12. Comping Practice with Roots

Practice 4.7. Combining II Minor 7♭5 with Dominant 7(♭9,♭13)

14

Minor 7♭5 Workout

Combine the minor 7♭5 from this chapter with a dominant 7 chord with altered tensions ♭9 and ♭13 (discussed in chapter 6). Use guide tones in the LH and UST ♭II minor in the RH for the dominant 7 chord. (Question: What other chord tone or tension remains in UST ♭II minor? Answer in chapter 6!)

You can use UST V major when the progression resolves. Try not to write out the voicings. You can, however, place the USTs above a horizontal line over each chord.

Minor 7♭5 Workout

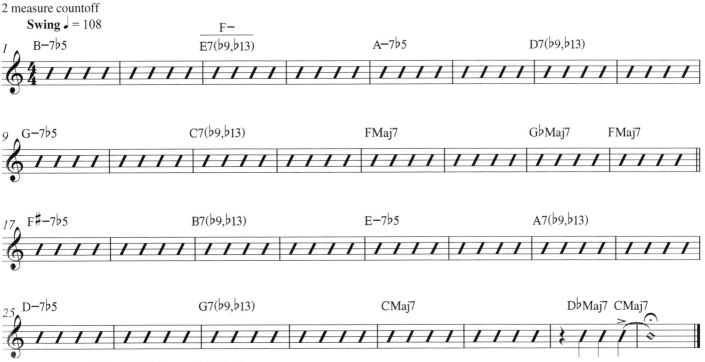

Fig. 4.13. Minor 7♭5 Workout

Practice 4.8. "Tune In"

15
with piano

16
without piano

Practice "Tune In" using the following approach.

1. Carefully analyze the chord sheet in figure 4.15. Note the "altered" dominant chords, and name the tensions. These chords will be discussed in chapter 6.

2. Listen to the piano on track 15.

3. Remember the most important part of comping is a smooth transition between the chords as they move through the progression.

4. Change inversions of the UST when the chord duration is the same for two measures, such as measures 4–5 and 7–8. For example, you can play the A triad in second inversion over the DMaj7 in measure 4.

5. Play through track 16 with your own comping style.

"Tune In" Lead Sheet

Fig. 4.14. "Tune In" Lead Sheet

"Tune In" Chord Sheet

Suzanna Sifter

After Piano Solo, D.C. al 2nd Ending to Coda

CODA

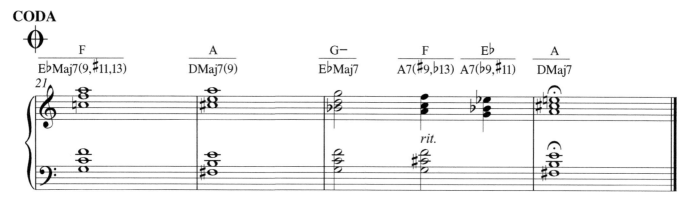

Fig. 4.15. "Tune In" Chord Sheet

At this point, we have studied the major 7, dominant 7, minor 7, and minor 7♭5 chords. Apply your knowledge of USTs *every time* you play a tune, whether in an ensemble, sessions, when practicing, or sight reading any lead sheets. Write in the horizontal lines, and place the appropriate tension specific UST over each chord symbol. Soon, you will be able to apply USTs to all chords, in any situation, and create rich sounding voicings!

Diminished 7

In chapter 5, we look at diminished 7 chords. The diminished 7 chord is unique in that it is built in three minor thirds. The root and ♭5 and the ♭3 and diminished 7 are both tritones.

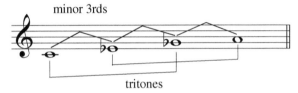

Fig. 5.1. Construction of Diminished 7 Chord

This dissonant and unstable sound creates motion in a chord progression because it wants to resolve. It is most often used as a passing chord between more stable sounds, creating tension and release. Suggested standards for practicing diminished 7 chord USTs are "Easy Living," "Rhythm Changes" (reharmonized), "Desafinado," and "Once I Loved." Diminished 7 chords are also used in more modern situations of long harmonic duration where the ear can explore the dissonant sounds of the chord tones mixed with varied tensions.

CHORD SCALE

The *combination diminished* scale (also called "symmetrical diminished") is comprised of two diminished chords a whole step apart. This creates an 8-note scale built in whole steps and half steps repeatedly until the root is again reached.

Fig. 5.2. The Symmetrical-Diminished Scale

Diminished 7 into Dominant 7

Diminished 7 chords are usually less familiar to the pianist because they are often reharmonized with a II V in more modern tunes. The tritones are easily used as the guide tones of a dominant 7.

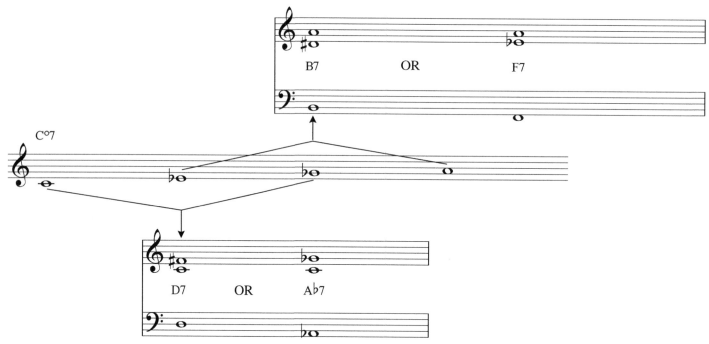

Fig. 5.3. Dominant 7 Guide Tones from a Diminished Chord

The diminished chord is a great sound and needs to be studied to create equal familiarity for complete seventh-chord knowledge. First, notice how diminished 7 chords are symmetrical: C°7, E♭°7, G♭°7, and A°7 (chord tones of a C°7 chord) are all the same diminished chord in different inversions.

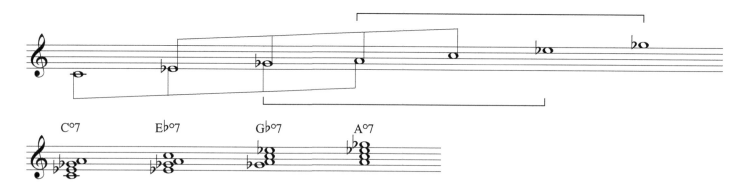

Fig. 5.4. The Diminished 7 Chord Is Symmetrical

The same is true for the chords built on the chord tones of C♯°7 and D°7. The next note up chromatically is E♭, which is the third of C°7, bringing us back to the C diminished family. Thus, there are really only three families of diminished chords: those built on C, C♯, and D. The remaining chords are inversions.

Practice 5.1. Learning the Diminished 7 Chord and Symmetrical-Diminished Scale

- Practice each diminished 7 chord in all family groups: C°7, C♯°7, and D°7.
- Always be conscious of the root of the chord you are studying, remaining aware of the inversions.
- Notice how there are only three different symmetrical-diminished scales. Others are the same scales, starting on different notes!
- Play the scales with the RH while comping a diminished 7 chord with syncopation in the LH.

Fig. 5.5. Symmetrical-Diminished Scale with LH Syncopation

The Passing-Diminished Scale

The passing-diminished chord scale set offers alternate chord scales for the diminished 7 chord. These scales are based on the chord tones of a diminished 7 with the remainder of the chord scale being diatonic to the key (also called "diatonic diminished"). The passing diminished chords are ♯I°7, ♯II°7, ♯IV°7, ♯V°7, and ♭III°7. For example, in the key of C, ♯I°7 is C♯°7. The notes of C♯°7 are: C♯, E, G, and B♭. The remainder of the notes will be from the C major scale: (C♯), D, (E), F, (G), A, (B♭), C.

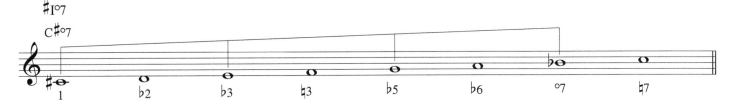

Fig. 5.6. C♯ Passing-Diminished Scale

To compare the tensions of the ♯I passing diminished and symmetrical-diminished scales, passing diminished offers a ♭9, 10 (major 3), ♭13, and 14 (major 7), while symmetrical diminished offers 9, 11, ♭13, and 14 (major 7).

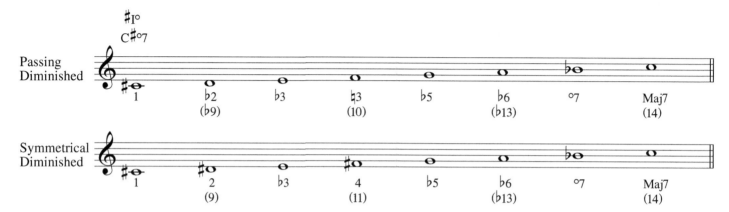

Fig. 5.7. Tension Comparison: Passing-Diminished and Symmetrical-Diminished Scales

The more commonly used tensions are 9, 11, and 14, which come from symmetrical diminished. We will use this scale as an example for the diminished 7 chord.

Exploring the passing-diminished chord-scale set offers many differing USTs to the pool of rich sounds coloring the diminished 7 chord. Write out each chord scale, and discover the possibilities!

THE LSTS AND USTS OF DIMINISHED 7: C♯°7

1. Write out the C♯ symmetrical-diminished scale.

Fig. 5.8. Symmetrical-Diminished Scale

2. Build triads diatonically on each scale degree. Note multiple triads on scale degrees 2, 4, ♭6, and natural 7.

Fig. 5.9. Symmetrical-Diminished Triads

3. Label each scale degree with a Roman numeral. Then analyze the chord quality, and state whether the triad is an LST or UST.

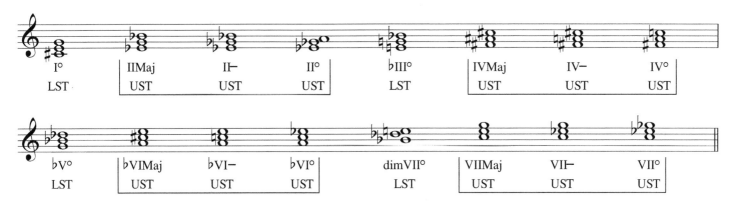

Fig. 5.10. C♯ Symmetrical-Diminished Triads: LSTs and USTs

Diminished 7 Triad Grid

Diminished 7 Chord: Symmetrical-Diminished Scale

LSTs	USTs		
1. I°	1. II(9)	5. IV–(11,♭13)	9. ♭VI°(♭13,14,9)
2. ♭III°	2. II–(9,11)	6. IV°(11,♭13,14)	10. VII(14)
3. ♭V°	3. II°(9,11,♭13)	7. ♭VI(♭13)	11. VII–(14,9)
4. dimVII°	4. IV(11)	8. ♭VI–(♭13,14)	12. VII°(14,9,11)

Fig. 5.11. Symmetrical-Diminished Triads

The LSTs for a diminished 7 chord are I°, ♭III°, ♭V°, and dimVII°.

In the case of symmetrical diminished, there are twelve USTs! These USTs range from one to three tensions in various orders as the triads rise in the scale.

The qualities of the triads that appear on the same scale degree are major, minor, and diminished. While many tension combinations exist in theory, they are not all equal to the ear! Applications of tensions depend on many parameters, such as melody, harmonic duration, placement of harmony in phrase/form, and previous/subsequent chords.

Particular care must be used when adding tensions to diminished 7 chords in standard chord progressions. A general rule is that when a chord is less stable, use less tensions, especially if the harmonic duration is short. For example, a harmonic duration of two beats as a passing diminished chord should take the least-obtrusive tension, which is the 11, or it may not take any tensions.

A typical longer-duration diminished sound involves the USTs VII major, ♭VI major, IV major, and II major over the root, diminished 7, flat 5, and flat 3, respectively.

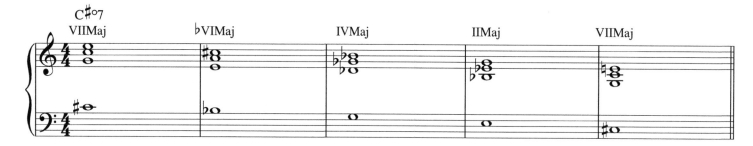

Fig. 5.12. Longer-Duration Diminished Harmonization

Tension Chart

To narrow the spectrum of USTs, use II major, IV major, or VII major. UST formulas for C°7 and F°7 are:

Indicated Tensions	UST	C°7	F°7
9	II	$\dfrac{D}{C°7}$	$\dfrac{G}{F°7}$
11	IV	$\dfrac{F}{C°7}$	$\dfrac{B\flat}{F°7}$
14	VII	$\dfrac{B}{C°7}$	$\dfrac{E}{F°7}$

Practice 5.2. UST Recognition Practice for Diminished 7

Write in the associated UST for each given chord. Remember, the three UST options for this exercise are II major, IV major, or VII major.

1. $\dfrac{\text{𝄞}}{A°7(9)}$	2. C°7(11)	3. E♭°7(14)	4. B°7(11)
5. C♯°7(14)	6. F°7(11)	7. E°7(11)	8. F♯°7(9)
9. E♭°7(11)	10. B♭°7(14)	11. G°7(9)	12. D♭°7(9)
13. B°7(9)	14. G♭°7(14)	15. B♭°7(9)	16. D♯°7(14)
17. F°7(11)	18. D°7(9)	19. A♭°7(11)	20. C°7(14)

DIMINISHED 7 VOICINGS

The LH voicing for the diminished 7 chord is LST I diminished, also used for the minor 7♭5 chord in chapter 4. When the UST contains the diminished 7 chord tone, the LH voicing does not have to contain the diminished seventh chord tone. In this case, LST I diminished works well as a LH voicing. However, when the UST does not contain the diminished 7 chord tone, the LH must contain the diminished 7 chord tone, as well as the ♭3 and ♭5, and potentially the root. Either play the ♭III diminished LST (any inversion) or the entire diminished 7 chord. For review, refer to the minor 7♭5 LH worksheet in chapter 4.

For example, the UST II major contains tension 9 along with the ♭5 and diminished 7 chord tones. In this case, the LH can use LST I diminished because the diminished 7 chord tone is in the RH.

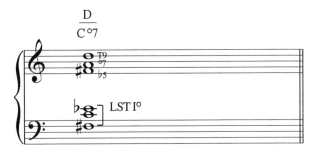

Fig. 5.13. LST I° (Second Inversion) with UST II Major

However, in the case of UST VII major (which contains ♭3, ♭5, and tension 14), the diminished 7 chord tone is not present in the RH. This means the LH chord sound must contain the diminished 7 chord tone, by playing LST ♭III. You have the option of using the root in the LH voicing in any inversion to give the chord more stability.

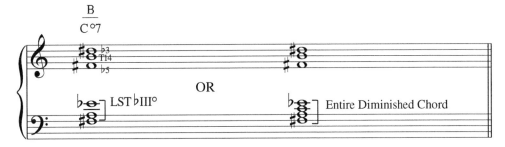

Fig. 5.14. LST ♭III° or I° 7 with UST VII Major

The presence of either the flat 7 or diminished 7 is very important because it distinguishes the minor 7♭5 from the diminished 7 chord.

Practice 5.3. Open-Position Voice Leading

Complete the open-position voicings in figure 5.15 using UST II major. Work with different inversions of the USTs. You can also practice UST VII major, with LST ♭III in the LH.

1. Write in chord symbols through the circle of fifths.

2. Write in USTs over the chord symbols.

3. Write out the LH voicings.

4. Write out USTs, using voice leading.

5. Practice, memorize, experiment!

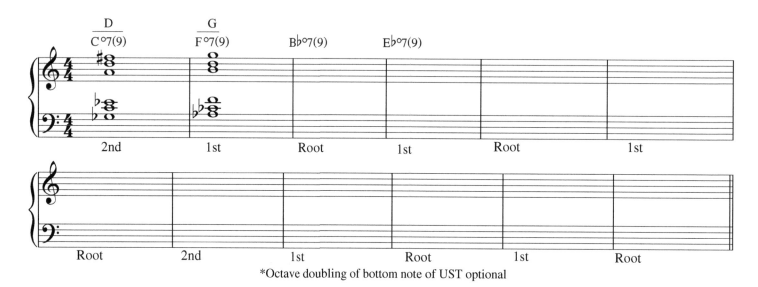

*Octave doubling of bottom note of UST optional

Fig. 5.15. Diminished 7 Open-Position Voicings. Note that these voicings are true polychords due to the full triad in the LH.

Practice 5.4. Comping Practice with Roots

Practice these voicings solo through the circle of fifths, in tempo, eight measures per key.

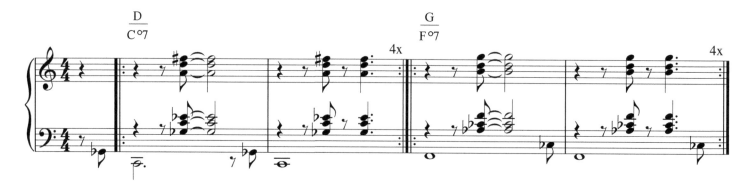

Fig. 5.16. Comping Practice with Roots

As always, be aware of the chord you are playing without getting confused by the root of the LST/ UST verses the root of the actual chord being played. During practice sessions, feel free to play the root in the lower register to anchor the chord.

Practice 5.5. Combined Diminished 7 Workout

17

Diminished 7 Workout

Combine your voicings from previous chapters to comp with your new diminished chords through the "Diminished 7 Workout." Fill in the USTs of your choice above each chord symbol, and strive to play the voicings without writing them out. You can play through the progression out of time at first and then add tempo with longer harmonic durations of each chord. Then play along with track 17.

Diminished 7 Workout

Fig. 5.17. Diminished 7 Workout

Practice 5.6. "Have We Met?"

18
with piano

19
without piano

Practice "Have We Met?" using the following approach.

1. Play each chord in figure 5.19 out of tempo, to really hear the voicing. Note the correlation between the USTs and the tensions.

2. Listen to track 18, and follow along with the piano as it accompanies the melody and improvisation.

3. Read through the chord sheet in figure 5.19, then create your own voicings. Start by inverting the given triads. Remember, you can voice lead the top note by step as a counter line.

4. Play along with track 19, and comp freely behind the saxophone.

"Have We Met?" Lead Sheet

Fig. 5.18. Lead sheet: "Have We Met?"

"Have We Met?" Chord Sheet

Form: 2 measure countoff
   Head In
   Sax Solo 1/2 Chorus
   Piano Solo B Section
   Head Out Last A
   To Coda

Fig. 5.19. "Have We Met?" Chord Sheet

While the diminished chord is used less frequently in jazz standards these days, it is a complex and colorful sound that adds forward motion to standard chord progressions. Experiment with progressions with longer duration diminished 7 chords. Use it as an interlude between choruses exploring different USTs.

CHAPTER 6

Alternate Scales and USTs of Dominant 7

CHORD SCALES

We are learning that USTs in jazz piano comping are an excellent way to add tensions to chords in an organized manner.

Every chord quality has several varied USTs, depending on the chord scale you choose. One chord quality might have up to seven chord scales from which various USTs are derived. This is especially true for the dominant 7 chord. If the chord symbol is G7(9,13) with natural tensions, then the chord scale must be Mixolydian, as Mixolydian is the only scale that contains those natural tensions where the I chord is dominant. However, when you choose altered tensions, the chord scales that reflect these tensions will be different.

The most common chord scales for the dominant 7 chords are:
- Mixolydian
- Mixolydian ♭9
- Mixolydian ♭9,♭13
- Lydian ♭7
- Altered
- Whole Tone
- Symmetrical Dominant
- Blues

First, let's take a look at the parent scales from which these chord scales are derived.

As we learned in chapter 1, Mixolydian is the fifth mode of the major scale. In the same way, Mixolydian ♭9 and Mixolydian ♭9,♭13 are the fifth modes of the harmonic-major (♭6) and harmonic-minor (♭3, ♭6) scales, respectively. Lydian ♭7 is the fourth mode, and altered (Superlocrian) is the seventh mode of the melodic-minor scale (♭3 only; see figure 6.1).

Spelling Altered Scale Degrees

Remember, all scale degree alterations refer to the major scale. For example, we say that Mixolydian includes "♭7," and Lydian ♭7 includes "♯4" and "♭7."

The I chord is dominant in Mixolydian, Lydian ♭7, and symmetrical dominant. The I chord in the altered and whole tone scales is *augmented* dominant: I+7.

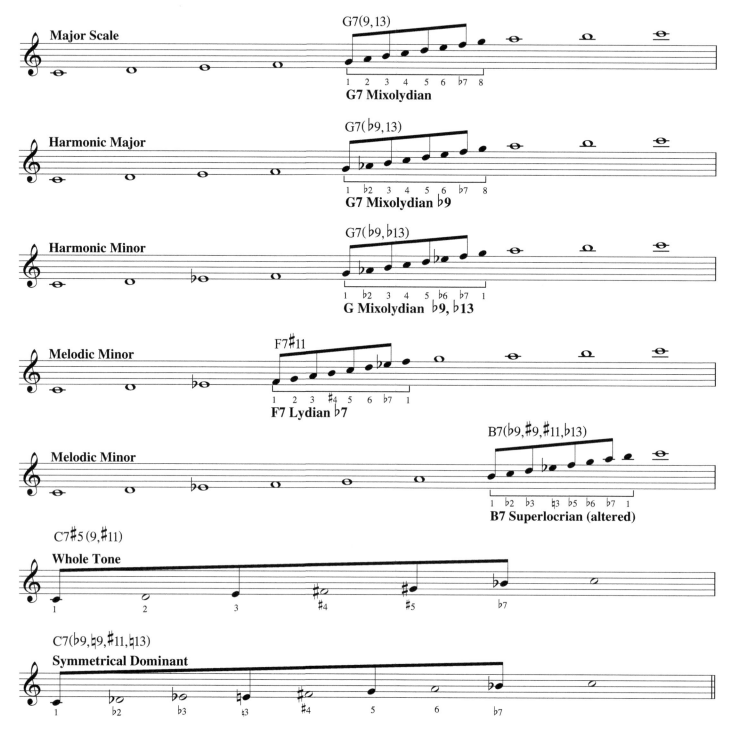

Fig. 6.1. Possible Chord Scales for Dominant 7

For dominant 7 chords, the form of the symmetrical scale is half step/whole step, symmetrical dominant (which is the opposite of symmetrical diminished; see chapter 5). You will again find that there are only three scale shapes; the remainder of scales are the same, just starting on a different note. So, the C, E♭, G♭, and A symmetrical-dominant scales are all the same scale starting on different scale degrees.

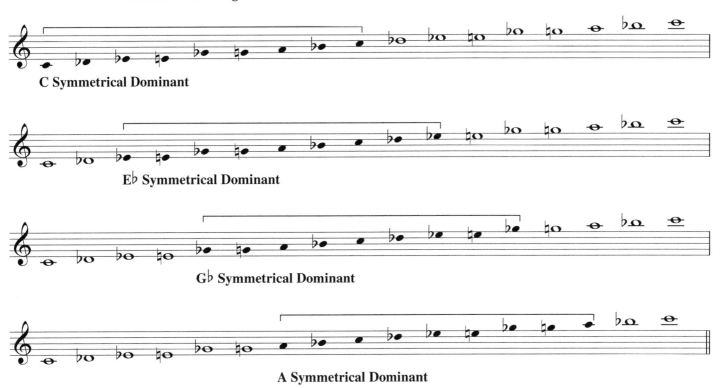

Fig. 6.2. Symmetrical-Dominant Scales from C, E♭, G♭, and A

Practice 6.1. Learning to Hear Altered Tensions on Dominant 7 Chords

1. Play a low G and the guide tones of a dominant 7 in mid register.

2. Let the chord ring, and play a tension (starting with ♭9) in the upper register.

3. Sing the tension, and resolve it to the nearest chord tone (in the case of ♭9, the root).

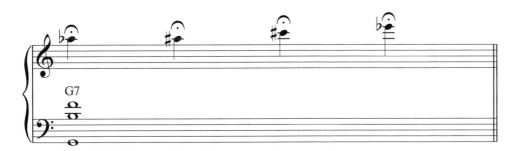

Fig. 6.3. Listening to Altered Tensions

4. Repeat this process with the following tensions and resolutions:
    *   Resolve ♭9 to the root.
    *   Resolve ♯9 to the 3rd.
    *   Resolve ♯11 to the 5th.
    *   Resolve ♭13 to the 5th.

Fig. 6.4. Resolving Altered Tensions to Chord Tones

5. Change keys and repeat the exercise.

Tips:
*   Use your inner hearing to sing an altered tension, and then play the tension to test for accuracy.
*   Experiment with playing and hearing tension combinations, such as (♭9,♭13), (♯9,♭13), and (♭9,♯11), both melodically and harmonically.
*   Combine altered tensions with natural tensions, such as (♭9,13) or (♭9,♯11,13), harmonically.
*   Sing and resolve each tension.

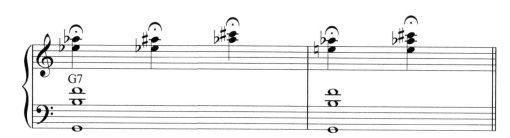

Fig. 6.5. Hearing Tension Combinations

ALTERED DOMINANT AND SYMMETRICAL-DOMINANT SCALES

In this chapter, we look at the altered and symmetrical-dominant scales because they are particularly rich in USTs. The first five notes of these scales are the same, expressing tensions ♭9, ♯9, and ♯11. Then, the altered scale continues up in whole tones, yielding tension ♭13, while the symmetrical dominant gives a natural 5 and 13 (see figure 6.6).

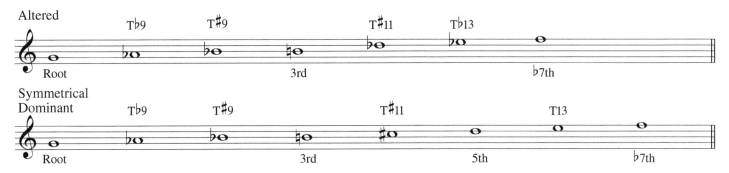

Fig. 6.6. Altered Compared to Symmetrical Dominant

Practice 6.2. Altered/Symmetrical Dominant Practice

Become familiar with these scales by playing through figure 6.7 in multiple keys. Keep in mind that the LH voicings must accurately reflect the scale's tensions. In this case, the difference between LH voicings is ♭13 or natural 13 (5).

Fig. 6.7. Altered and Symmetrical-Dominant Scale/Comping Exercises

USTS OF DOMINANT 7 USING THE ALTERED SCALE

When working with the altered and symmetrical-dominant scales, be aware that there may be two or three triads per scale degree. For example, in the altered scale, the I chord can be either augmented or diminished. Watch for enharmonics: an E♭ can be seen as a D♯, which is the 3rd degree of the B altered scale (III augmented).

To find the LSTs and USTs for a G7 chord using the altered scale:

1. Write out the G altered scale, and build triads diatonically on each scale degree. Note multiple triads on scale degrees 1 and ♭6. Label each scale degree with a Roman numeral. Then analyze the chord quality and state whether the triad is an LST or UST.

Fig. 6.8. G Altered Triads: USTs

2. Fill in the Altered/Dominant Triad Grid. In this case, all triads are USTs! Memorize the varied tension(s) within the Roman numerals.

Dominant 7 Chord: Altered Scale

LSTs	USTs	
None	1. I+(♭13)	6. ♭V(♭9,♯11)
	2. I°(♯9,♯11)	7. ♭VI(♯9,♭13)
	3. ♭II−(♭9,♭13)	8. ♭VI+(♭13)
	4. ♭III−(♯9,♯11)	9. ♭VII°(♭9)
	5. III+(♭13)	

Fig. 6.9. Altered/Dominant Triad Grid

Tension Chart

All triads for the altered scale are USTs because the #5 is also considered a b13. The I+, III+, and bVI+ are all the same triad, inverted, containing Tb13. The I° triad offers T#9 and T#11, and bVII° contains Tb9. The most important USTs for the altered scale are bII minor, bIII minor, bV major, and bVI major.

The USTs you choose must be tension specific. If the chord symbol states dominant 7(b9,b13), the UST *must* be bII minor. Similarly, when the chord symbol states dominant 7(#9, #11), the UST is bIII minor. To narrow the UST possibilities, use bII minor, bIII minor, bV major, and bVI major. UST formulas for C7(alt) and F7(alt) are:

Indicated Tensions	UST	C7	F7
b9,b13	bII–	Db–⁄C7(alt)	Gb–⁄F7(alt)
#9,#11	bIII–	Eb–⁄C7(alt)	Ab–⁄F7(alt)
b9,#11	bV	Gb⁄C7(alt)	B⁄F7(alt)
#9,b13	bVI	Ab⁄C7(alt)	Db⁄F7(alt)

Practice 6.3. UST Recognition Practice for Altered Dominant

Write in the tension-specific UST over each chord: bII minor, bIII minor, bV major, and bVII major. Play each chord, and work at developing instant recognition!

1. **Ab–**⁄G7(b9,b13)	2. Eb7(#9,#11)	3. C#7(b9,#11)	4. F7(#9,b13)
5. Bb7(#9,#11)	6. Db7(#9,b13)	7. D7(b9,b13)	8. F#7(b9,#11)
9. C7(b9,b13)	10. Gb7(#9,#11)	11. A7(b9,#11)	12. B7(#9,b13)
13. Ab7(b9,#11)	14. E7(#9,#11)	15. F#7(b9,b13)	16. Eb7(#9,b13)
17. C7(#9,#11)	18. Bb7(b9,b13)	19. E7(b9,#11)	20. Db7(#9,#11)

LSTs AND USTs OF DOMINANT 7 USING THE SYMMETRICAL-DOMINANT SCALE

Build triads, and label the LSTs and USTs using the symmetrical-dominant scale.

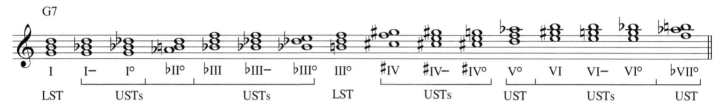

Fig. 6.10. LSTs and USTs Using the Symmetrical-Dominant Scale

Dominant 7 Chord: Symmetrical-Dominant Scale

LSTs	USTs	
1. I	1. I–(♯9)	8. ♯IV–(♭9,♯11,13)
2. III°	2. I°(♯9,♯11)	9. ♯IV°(♯11,13)
	3. ♭II°(♭9)	10. V°(♭9)
	4. ♭III(♯9)	11. VI(♭9,13)
	5. ♭III–(♯9,♯11)	12. VI–(13)
	6. ♭III°(♯9,♯11,13)	13. VI°(♯9,13)
	7. ♯IV(♭9,♯11)	14. ♭VII°(♭9)

Fig. 6.11. Symmetrical-Diminished Grid

Because the symmetrical-dominant scale contains a natural 5, it has two LSTs: I major and III diminished. The most commonly used USTs for the symmetrical-dominant scale are VI major (♭9, 13) and ♯IV minor (♭9,♯11,13). These triads can be used as a bright sound on the V7 chord in a minor key, even though they contain natural 13. The VI major is also available. However, there is no distinction between altered and symmetrical dominant when the 13 is not in the voicing.

When committing to a particular sound, it works best to feature the characteristic notes of the scales that differentiate the sounds. The most commonly used UST formulas for the dominant 7 chord using the symmetrical-dominant scale on a C7 and F7 are:

Indicated Tensions	UST	C7	F7
♭9,♯11,13	♯IV–	F♯– C7(♭9,♯11,13)	B– F7(♭9,♯11,13)
♭9,13	VI	A C7(♭9,13)	D F7(♭9,13)

Practice 6.4. UST Recognition Practice for Symmetrical Dominant

Write in the tension-specific UST over each chord, and play them.

1. $\overline{A}$ C7(♭9,13)	2. A♭7(♭9,♯11,13)	3. B7(♭9,13)	4. E♭7(♭9,♯11,13)
5. E♭7(♭9,13)	6. D♭7(♭9,13)	7. A7(♭9,13)	8. F7(♯11,13)
9. F♯7(♭9,♯11,13)	10. B♭7(♭9,♯11,13)	11. D7(♭9,13)	12. C♯7(♭9,13)
13. E7(♭9,♯11,13)	14. G♭7♭9,♯11,13)	15. F7(♭9,13)	16. B♭7(♭9,13)
17. D♭7(♭9,♯11,13)	18. E7(♭9,13)	19. D7(♭9,♯11,13)	20. G7(♭9,13)

To complete your knowledge of all possible UST combinations on a dominant 7 chord, follow the same process with the Mixolydian ♭9; Mixolydian ♭9,♭13; Lydian ♭7; blues; and whole-tone scales.

VOICINGS

The following list shows the LH voicings for dominant 7 chords and their corresponding chord scales:

LH Voicing	Corresponding Chord Scales
1. Guide Tones	all chord scales
2. 3 ♭7 9	Mixolydian/Lydian ♭7
3. 3 ♭7 ♭9	Symmetrical Dominant/Altered/Mixolydian ♭9
4. 3 ♭7 ♯9	Symmetrical Dominant /Altered/Blues
5. ♭7 3 5	Mixolydian/Symmetrical Dominant/Mixolydian ♭9
6. ♭7 3 13	Mixolydian/Symmetrical Dominant/Lydian ♭7
7. ♭7 3 ♭13	Altered/Mixolydian ♭9,♭13

Choose the UST based on the difference between the USTs, rather than the similarities.

Practice 6.5 LH Voicings

Review the LH voicings from chapter 2, and then practice the voicings in figure 6.12 through the circle of fifths.

- In first inversion, use 3, ♭7, and ♭9 or ♯9.
- In third inversion, use either ♭7, 3, ♭13 or ♭7, 3, 13.
- Optionally, use four-note voicings (GT + 2). Be careful not to include an excess of doubled chord tones or tensions in open-position voicings.

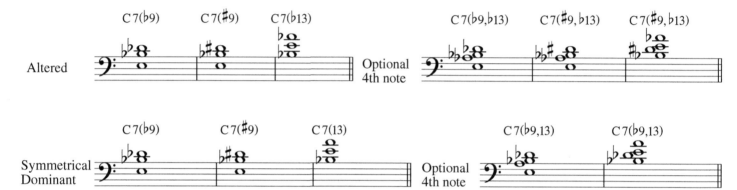

Fig. 6.12. LH Voicings for Altered and Symmetrical Dominant

Practice 6.6. Altered Dominant with USTs

Next, add ♭V major/♭VI major or ♭II minor/♭III minor to the altered LH voicings. Refer to figures 6.13 and 6.14. Fill out the voicings. Practice each voicing separately as a vamp, changing the inversions as you hear them. Also, play altered voicings with coupling triads. Transpose them through the circle of fifths, and commit them to memory.

Altered Voicings 1: ♭V, ♭VI Major

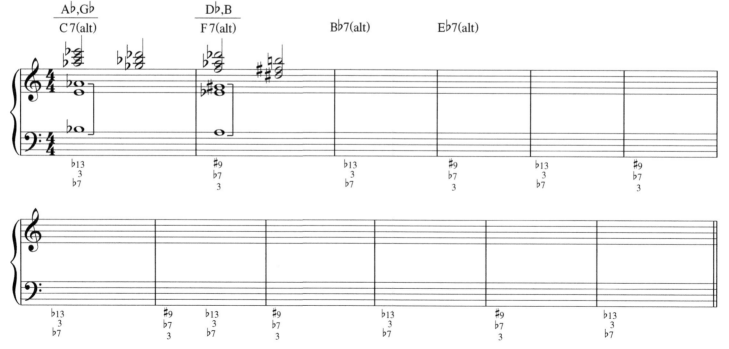

Fig. 6.13. Altered Dominant 7 Open-Position Voicings 1: ♭V Major and ♭VI Major

Altered Voicings 2: ♭II–, ♭III–

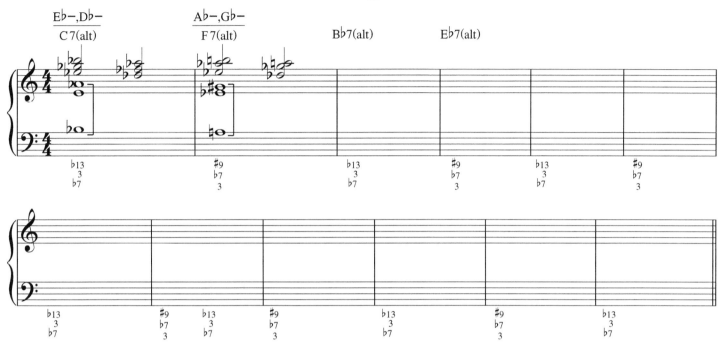

Fig. 6.14. Altered Dominant 7 Open-Position Voicings 2: ♭II– and ♭III–

Practice 6.7. Symmetrical Dominant with USTs

Next, add VI major or ♯IV minor to the symmetrical-dominant LH voicings. Make sure to use another natural 13 or 5 in the LH voicing. Work with these new sounds to train your ear, and commit them to memory.

Symmetrical-Dominant Voicings 1: VI Major

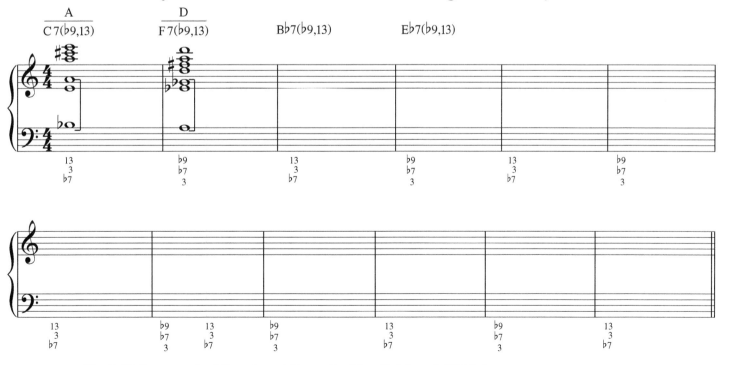

Fig. 6.15. Symmetrical-Dominant Open-Position Voicings 1: VI Major

Symmetrical-Dominant Voicings 2: ♯IV–

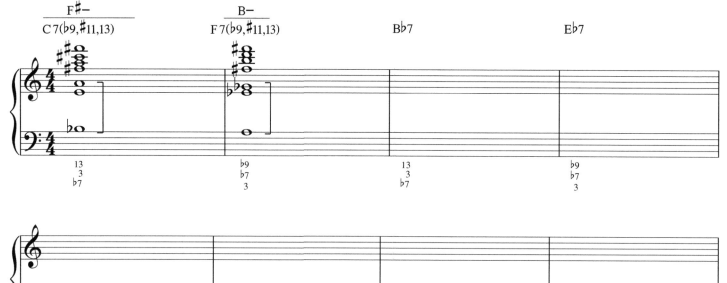

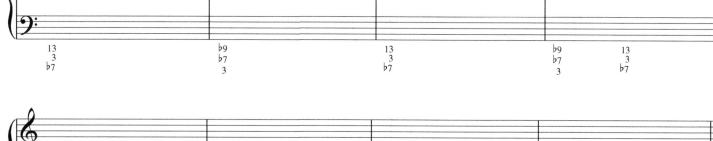

Fig. 6.16. Symmetrical-Dominant Open-Position Voicings 2: ♯IV Minor

Practice 6.8. Comping Practice with Roots

Practice these voicings, without accompaniment, through the circle of fifths, in tempo, eight measures per key.

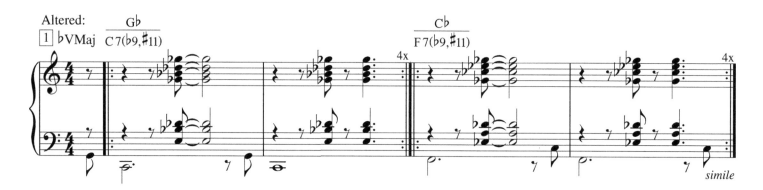

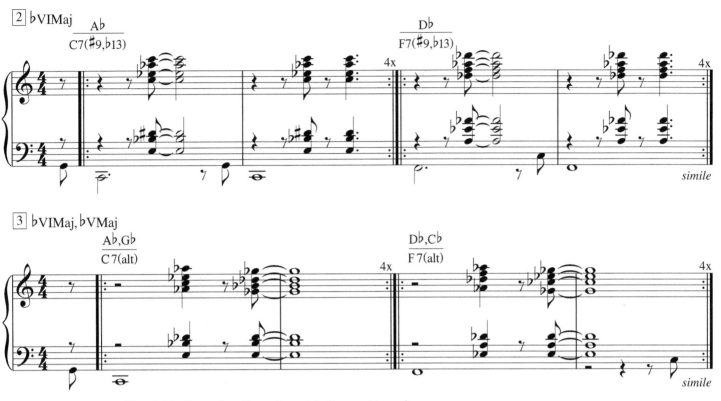

Fig. 6.17. Comping Practice with Roots: Altered

Fig. 6.18. Solo Symmetrical-Dominant Voicing Exercises

While eventually all possibilities should be explored, at first, stay with the major and minor USTs. The major and minor triads are more stable than the augmented and diminished triads, but it's all about the sound you want.

Practice 6.9. Altered Dominant Pedal Workout

20
with piano

21
without piano

On track 20, listen to the piano comp altered voicings over a tonic *pedal* (rhythmically repeated root of each chord). Notice how the USTs color the chords and add motion to the bass pedal.

Use track 21 (without piano) to move the altered USTs over this pedal. Shift between the USTs as your ear hears them. Vary the rhythms, range, LH, and USTs of your voicings.

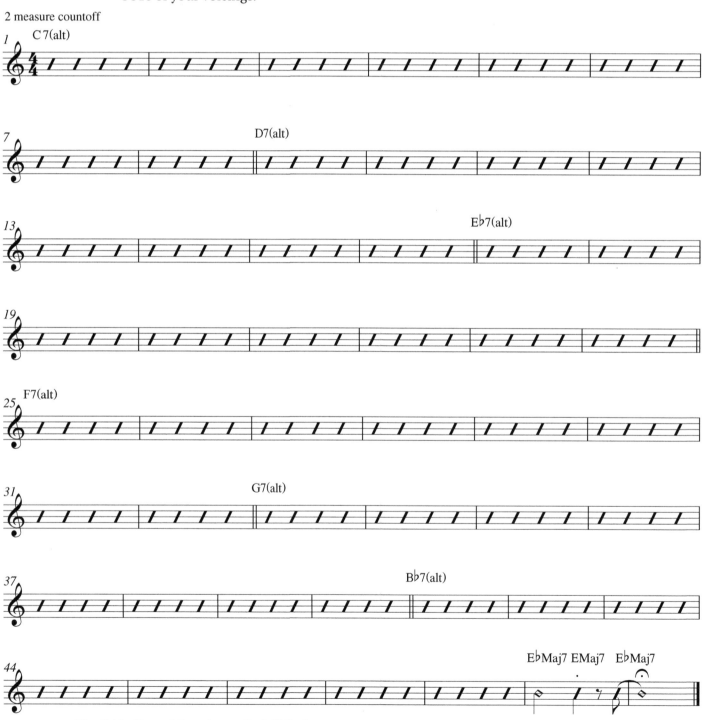

Fig. 6.19. Altered Dominant Pedal Workout

Practice 6.10. Symmetrical-Dominant Workout

22

Combine the new symmetrical-dominant voicings from this chapter, and resolve down to a minor 7 chord with track 22. Use the UST of your choice for I–7. You can practice your LH voicings first, and then add the USTs. The progression moves down in whole steps (twice to reach all twelve keys).

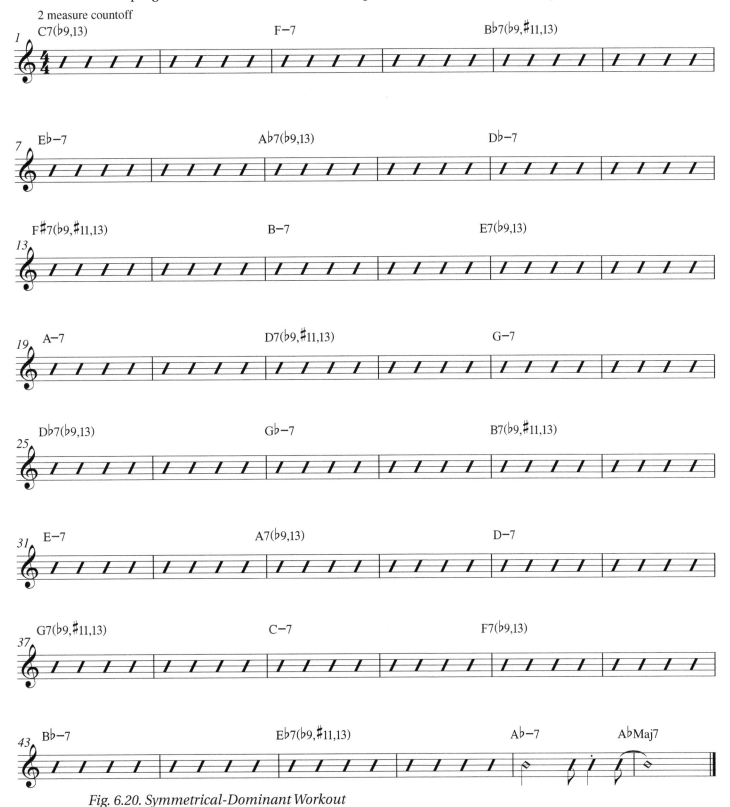

Fig. 6.20. Symmetrical-Dominant Workout

Practice 6.11. "Out Tune"

23
with piano

24
without piano

"Out Tune" is a reharmonized version of "Tune In." It incorporates most USTs studied in this book! Read through the chord sheet in figure 6.22, slowly and carefully. You may find it helpful to analyze the voicings by writing in the chord tones and tensions for each voicing. You can also analyze the melody based on the chord of the moment. Use practice techniques such as vamping on one chord, one measure, two measures, etc., in tempo. The small rhythmic notation in measures 10 to 12 indicate the rhythm to comp with during the melody. Listen to the pianist's interpretation on track 23. When you are ready, play along with track 24.

"Out Tune" Lead Sheet

Form: 2 measure countoff
  Head
  Sax 1/2 Chorus
  Piano 1/2 Chorus
  D.S. al ⊕
  Into ending ⊕

Fig. 6.21. Lead Sheet: "Out Tune"

"Out Tune" Chord Sheet

After Piano, D.S. al Coda

Fig. 6.22. "Out Tune" Chord Sheet

Practice 6.12. "Suz Blues"

25
with piano

26
without piano

"Suz Blues" is a 12-bar blues with altered chords, using a dominant pedal (5th degree in bass) in the first three bars. All of the altered USTs studied in this chapter can color these dominant 7 chords and can be used interchangeably during the solo section. The small rhythmic notation written above the lines of the lead sheet are kicks for the rhythm section, meant to be played during the melody. When playing in a trio, the kicks will work with just the LH. Remember, in the first three bars, you are playing F7(alt), not a C chord.

Practice "Suz Blues" using the following approach:

1. Analyze the written voicings in the piano part (Fig. 6.24) by placing the numeral of each chord or tension next to each note. Base this analysis on the chord of the moment rather than the key of the song.

2. Play each chord one at a time, and experiment with the sounds in order to really hear the voicings. Add the root in the lower register to anchor the sound. (You will not need the root when you play with a bassist.)

3. Listen to the arrangement, focusing on the piano, on track 25.

4. Play with the "music minus one" track 26.

5. Have fun!

Suz Blues

Form: Head in 2x
    Sax Solo 4x
    Piano Solo 2x
    Head out to

Fig. 6.23. Lead Sheet: "Suz Blues"

"Suz Blues" Piano Part

Fig. 6.24. Piano Part "Suz Blues"

Comping the dominant 7 chord requires a vast knowledge of tensions and tension combinations. The sounds immensely differ and offer many possibilities for the colors you hear and seek to play. Continue to listen carefully to these voicings by letting each chord sustain and singing the various tensions. Each tension and tension combination has its own sound, and the shading of a tension changes depending on the other tensions in the voicing and chord quality. For instance, a ♭9 sounds different with a 13 or a ♭13.

Harmonic context also effects the sound of tensions: a natural 13 on a V7 chord sounds different in a major key than in a minor key. Experiment with the sounds, and train your ear for instant recognition, in the same way as you memorize the UST formulas and the tensions they contain.

Chapter 7 will focus on twelve sets of possible combinations of USTs over a II V I progression!

The II V I Progression

You have now studied all chord types separately. We now apply our knowledge of USTs to the common II V I chord progression. Standards for practicing II V's include "Afternoon in Paris," "Tune Up," "Cherokee," "Airegin," and many others.

PERMUTATIONS

The following pages show the permutations of various USTs over the chords in major and minor II V I progressions. Alternate chord scales include Lydian ♭7, whole tone, and melodic minor. There are twelve sets of permutations, eight variations in each. Considering twelve keys, range of voicings, inversions, octave doublings, and context, the number of possibilities are immense!

Procedure for Permutation Practice

The chord scales from which the triads originate head each column. Each row is a set of USTs for each chord of the II V I progression.

1. Voice lead a LH voicing below the listed II V I. Make sure the tension(s) in the LH correspond to the UST!

2. Play each corresponding UST above the LH of the II V I voicing across each column.

3. Try each UST series in various keys and inversions.

Take your time, and make your way through each permutation. Repeat for subsequent permutations.

Permutation 1

II Dorian	V Mixolydian	I Ionian
RH Triads:		
(V– ♭VII)	(V– VI–)	(V VI–)
A–	D–	G
A–	E–	A–
A–	D–	A–
A–	E–	G
C	D–	G
C	E–	A–
C	D–	A–
C	E–	G
D–7	**G7**	**CMaj6/Maj7**

Permutation 2

II Dorian	V Mixolydian	I Lydian
RH Triads:		
(V– ♭VII)	(V– VI–)	(II VII–)
A–	D–	D
A–	E–	B–
A–	D–	B–
A–	E–	D
C	D–	D
C	E–	B–
C	D–	B–
C	E–	D
D–7	**G7**	**CMaj7**

Permutation 3

II Dorian	V Altered	I Ionian
RH Triads:		
(V– ♭VII)	(♭V ♭VI)	(V VI–)
A–	D♭	G
A–	E♭	A–
A–	D♭	A–
A–	E♭	G
C	D♭	G
C	E♭	A–
C	D♭	A–
C	E♭	G
D–7	**G7**	**CMaj6/Maj7**

Permutation 4

II Dorian	V Altered	I Lydian
RH Triads:		
(V– ♭VII)	(♭V ♭VI)	(II VII–)
A–	D♭	D
A–	E♭	B–
A–	D♭	B–
A–	E♭	D
C	D♭	D
C	E♭	B–
C	D♭	B–
C	E♭	D
D–7	**G7**	**CMaj7**

Permutation 5

II Dorian	V Symmetrical Dominant	I Ionian
RH Triads:		
(V– ♭VII)	(♯IV– VI)	(V VI–)
A–	C♯–	G
A–	E	A–
A–	C♯–	A–
A–	E	G
C	C♯–	G
C	E	A–
C	C♯–	A–
C	E	G
D–7	**G7**	**CMaj6/Maj7**

Permutation 6

II Dorian	V Symmetrical Dominant	I Lydian
RH Triads:		
(V– ♭VII)	(♯IV– VI)	(II VII–)
A–	C♯–	D
A–	E	B–
A–	C♯–	B–
A–	E	D
C	C♯–	D
C	E	B–
C	C♯–	B–
C	E	D
D–7	**G7**	**CMaj7**

Permutation 7

II Dorian	V Lydian ♭7	I Lydian
RH Triads:		
(V– ♭VII)	(II ♭VII+)	(II VII–)
A–	F+	D
A–	A	B–
A–	F+	B–
A–	A	D
C	F+	D
C	A	B–
C	F+	B–
C	A	D
D–7	**G7**	**CMaj7**

Permutation 8

II Dorian	V Whole Tone	I Ionian
RH Triads:		
(V– ♭VII)	(II aug III aug)	(V VI–)
A–	A+	G
A–	B+	A–
A–	A+	A–
A–	B+	G
C	A+	G
C	B+	A–
C	A+	A–
C	B+	G
D–7	**G7**	**CMaj6/Maj7**

Permutation 9

II Dorian	V Whole Tone	I Lydian
RH Triads:		
(V– ♭VII)	(II aug III aug)	(II VII–)
A–	A+	D
A–	B+	B–
A–	A+	B–
A–	B+	D
C	A+	D
C	B+	B–
C	A+	B–
C	B+	D
D–7	**G7**	**CMaj7**

Permutation 10

II Locrian (natural 9)	V Altered	I Melodic Minor
RH Triads:		
(♭VII)	(♭V ♭VI)	(IV V)
C	D♭	F
C	E♭	G
C	D♭	G
C	E♭	F
C	D♭	F
C	E♭	G
C	D♭	G
C	E♭	F
D–7♭5	**G7**	**C–(Maj6/Maj7)**

Permutation 11

II Locrian (Nat 9,13)	Altered	I Lydian
RH Triads:		
(IV ♭VII)	(♭V ♭VI)	(V VI–)
G	D♭	D
G	E♭	B–
G	D♭	B–
G	E♭	D
C	D♭	D
C	E♭	B–
C	D♭	B–
C	E♭	D
D–7♭5	**G7**	**CMaj7**

Permutation 12

I Ionian/Lydian	♯I Symmetrical Diminished	II Dorian	V Altered/Symmetrical Dominant
RH Triads:			
(II V)	(II IV VII)	(V– ♭VII)	(♭V ♭VI ♭II– VI)
G	E♭	A–	D♭
D	E♭	C	E♭
G	C	C	A♭–
G	G♭	A–	E
CMaj7	**C♯°7**	**D–7**	**G7**

The permutations are a pool of possibilities. Once you are familiar with the process, it will become easier to navigate the options.

Practice 7.1. II V I Workout

27

Work your way through twelve keys of the II V I progression. Use your choice of USTs. Allow your ear to smoothly guide you and voice lead through the progressions. Work at playing the chords at or close to the downbeat at the point of chord change. Look ahead in the music to prepare for the following chord.

II V I Workout

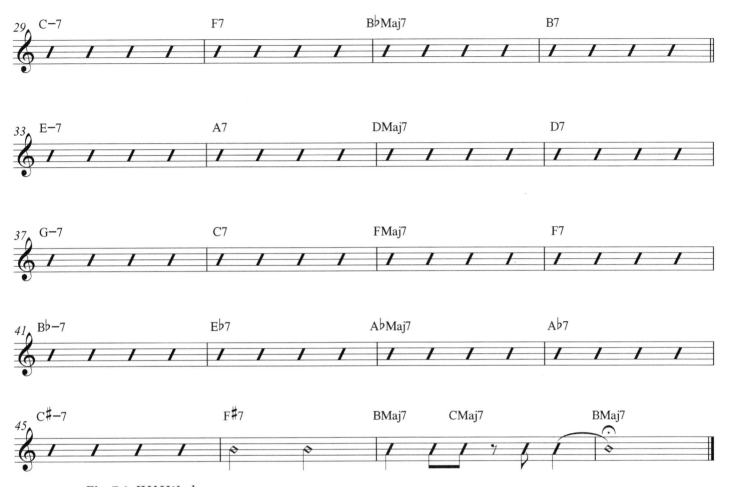

Fig. 7.1. II V I Workout

Practice 7.2. Flowers for You

28
with piano

29
without piano

"Flowers for You" is the title cut on my album *Flowers for You*. Practice this tune using the following approach:

1. Analyze the chord symbols on the lead sheet in figure 7.2 in terms of tension-specific USTs.

2. Write in the USTs above the chord symbols.

3. Compare your choices with the chord sheet, figure 7.3.

4. Listen to how the piano supports the bass, playing the melody on track 28.

5. Comp along with track 29. You may play different USTs during the solo section.

Note: Inversions and triads over bass tones use a forward slash mark in notation, e.g. F/G.

"Flowers for You" Lead Sheet

Suzanna Sifter

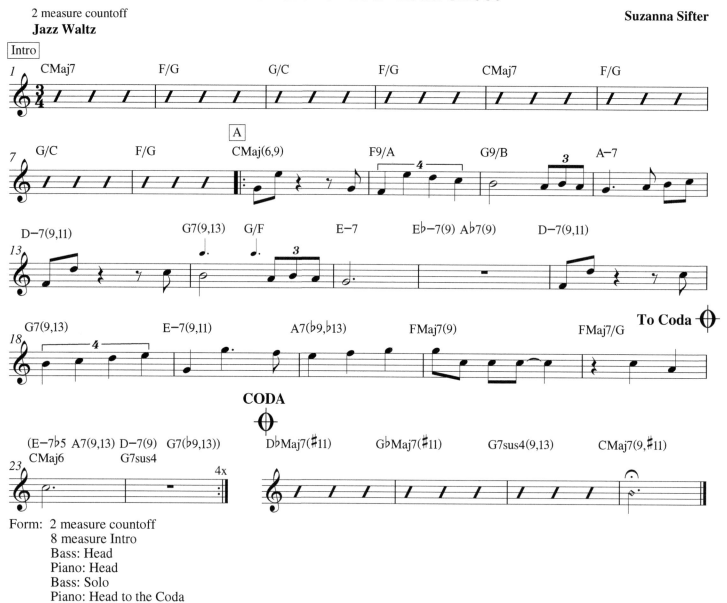

Fig. 7.2. "Flowers for You" Lead Sheet

Form: 2 measure countoff
8 measure Intro
Bass: Head
Piano: Head
Bass: Solo
Piano: Head to the Coda

"Flowers for You" Chord Sheet

Suzanna Sifter

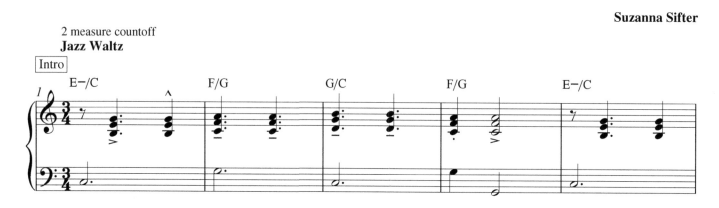

Fig. 7.3. "Flowers for You" Chord Sheet

The good news is that once you learn a triad—for example, C major—it can be used as an LST or UST over at least fifteen different seventh chords! Discover your favorite sounds, and build your own comping vocabulary.

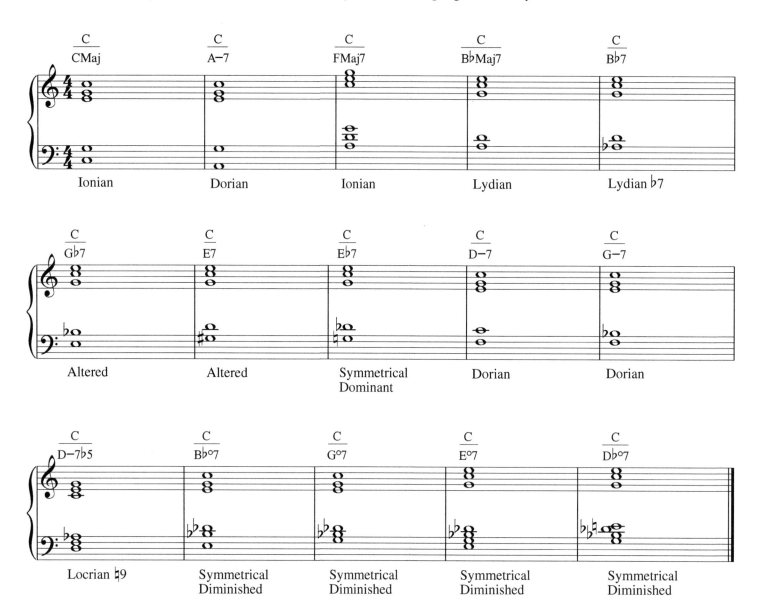

Fig. 7.4. Multiple Seventh Chord Options for the Major UST

Immediately write in the USTs above the primary chord symbol in all lead sheets you encounter. When you are familiar with the LH voicings and all triads in multiple keys and inversions, you will have great success at comping chords quickly with wider harmonic complexity. Eventually, you will be able to play any single voicing or II V I chord progression in a multitude of ways. A good beginner's goal is three to four different ways.

Once many permutations of the chords are memorized, you can begin to let your ear guide you through a chord progression as you hear the textures. This is a much higher level of expression than just playing voicings by sight, intellect, or rote. Become a sensitive, responsive, and supportive accompanist. Enjoy!

APPENDIX A

Alternate UST Applications

USTs are a valuable tool in four important ways: comping, harmonizing melodies, and melodic material for linear and harmonic improvisation. The following examples show melodic harmonization and melodic composition using USTs.

Blues for A.D.

"Blues for A.D." was written for the late, great jazz drummer, Alan Dawson. I recorded it on my CD *Flowers for You*.

Blues for A.D.

Suzanna Sifter

Here's "Blues for A.D." with the melody harmonized using USTs.

"Blues for A.D." Melody Harmonized

Suzanna Sifter

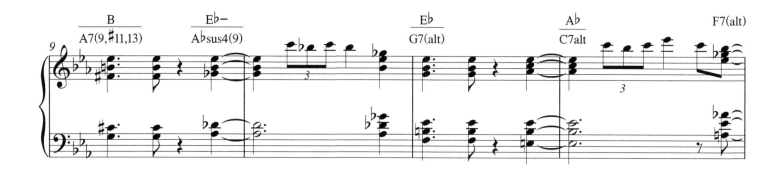

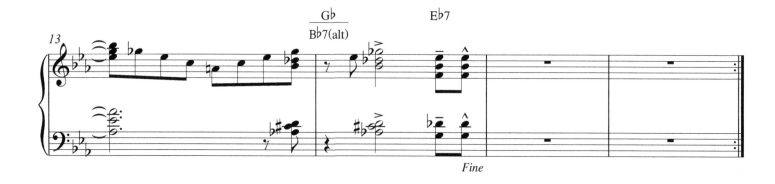

Fine

Lines for Charlie

"Lines for Charlie" is written in honor of the great jazz guru Charlie Banacos. On this lead sheet, slurs indicate USTs and numerals indicate scale degrees of the USTs. This tune is a good example of USTs being used linearly. It is recorded on my CD *Flowers for You*.

Lines for Charlie

Suzanna Sifter

Here is a chord worksheet for "Lines for Charlie." Use this form for the melody. Write out the extended harmonic rhythms for solo sections (8 measures each for first 3 chords). Use inversions of triads, and comp freely, interpreting varied tensions as you hear them. Voice lead at the points of chord changes.

"Lines for Charlie"
Chord Worksheet

Suzanna Sifter

Dark Eyes

"Dark Eyes" involves advanced harmonies, mixing various USTs with different expanded chord qualities. In this case, the USTs that are written in the lead sheet steer you towards an arrangement of specific voicings (see page 106). I recorded a solo piano version of "Dark Eyes" on my CD *The Illumination*.

"Dark Eyes" Lead Sheet

Suzanna Sifter

"Dark Eyes" Chord Sheet

Ad lib rhythm throughout

Suzanna Sifter

Glossary

These definitions describe how these terms are used in this book.

available tensions tensions that add color to the voicing without losing chord sound (chord quality)

avoid note an unavailable tension, or a note that conflicts with the basic structure of a seventh chord, such as the fourth on a major 7 chord

chord quality type of chord such as major 7 or dominant 7

chord scales various scales and modes that accompany seventh chords, such as Ionian for major 7 chords and Mixolydian for dominant 7 chords

chord sound tones comprised of the root, 3, 5, and 7, which express the quality of the chord

circle of fifths a succession of chords up or down in fifths through twelve keys (roots C F B♭ E♭ A♭ D♭ G♭ B E A D G)

comping a shortened term for the word "accompaniment;" playing chords in the LH or both hands in a group setting

coupling triads a combination of an LST and UST or two USTs a step apart, used over one seventh chord

guide tones the 3rd and 7th of a seventh chord

harmonic rhythm number of beats or measures of a chord in a harmonic progression

hybrid a triad over a bass note other than the root, 3, or 5 of the triad, separated by a slash mark such as G/C

"inside" (stable) notes that express only chord sound (1, 3, 5, 7); may be used harmonically or melodically

intervals the name of the spaces between musical tones, such as major or minor 3rds and perfect intervals such as the 4th and 5th

inversion triads/seventh chords played in any position: 1 3 5, 3 5 1, 5 1 3 or 1 3 5 7, 3 5 7 1, 5 7 1 3, 7 1 3 5

lead sheet music notation including melody and chord symbols

LH left hand

low interval limit the lowest a 3rd or 7th should be played harmonically in the LH voicing; in most situations, the E or D below middle C

LST any major, minor, augmented, or diminished triad comprised only of chord tones (1 3 5 or 3 5 7)

modal	a chord progression with the mode of a parent scale, such as Dorian, serving as the key
octave doubling	when playing a UST, doubling the bottom note an octave higher
open-position voicing	any voicing that spans more than an octave, such as superimposing a UST with the RH over a 3-note voicing in the LH
"outside" (less stable)	notes that express only tensions or out-of-key playing (♭9, ♯9, ♯11, ♭13, and chromatics); may be used harmonically or melodically
pedal	bass note remains constant under chords moving above
RH	right hand
Roman numeral formula method	the labeling of each LST and UST as a Roman Numeral; to memorize tensions as a formula in order to place over seventh chords
rootless voicing	a voicing which does not contain chord tone 1 (scale degree 1), the root; often used in group playing where there is a bass player; LH voicings often in first or third inversion substituting T9 for 1
scale degree	numerical name of the succession of tones in a scale
seventh chords	a chord containing the seventh note of its chord scale, such as 1 3 5 7 of Ionian, 1 3 5 ♭7 of Mixolydian, or 1 ♭3 5 ♭7 of Dorian
swing feel	quarter notes subdivided by eighth-note triplets; second eighth note placement on third triplet
tension combinations	two or more tensions in a voicing at once, such as ♭9, ♭13 or 9, ♯11, 13
tension substitution	9 replaces 1, and 13 replaces 5
tensions	tones a half or whole step above or below chord tones (♭9, 9, ♯9, 11, ♯11, 13, ♭13)
tonal	a chord progression with a parent scale, such as Ionian, serving as the key
triad qualities	major (1, 3, 5), minor (1, ♭3, 5), augmented (1, 3, ♯5), or diminished (1, ♭3, ♭5); *all alterations of chord tones based on the 1st, 3rd, and 5th of the major scale*
triads	a 3-note musical chord structured in thirds
unavailable tensions	tensions which obscure the 3rd or 7th of a chord, often creating a ♭9 with the guide tones
UST	any major, minor, augmented, or diminished triad that contains one or more tensions when superimposed over a seventh chord
vamp	a set chord progression which repeats until cue
voice leading	keeping the notes in common between two chords or stepwise motion at the point of chord change; minimal motion
voicing	various combinations of notes in a chord played harmonically, such as 4-way-close (LH) or open position (both hands)

Answer Key

Practice 1.3. UST Recognition Practice for Major 7

1.	$\dfrac{B}{\text{EMaj7(9)}}$	2.	$\dfrac{F\sharp-}{\text{GMaj7(9,}\sharp\text{11)}}$	3.	$\dfrac{E}{\text{DMaj7(9,}\sharp\text{11,13)}}$	4.	$\dfrac{G-}{\text{A}\flat\text{Maj7(9,}\sharp\text{11)}}$
5.	$\dfrac{C}{\text{FMaj7(9)}}$	6.	$\dfrac{C}{\text{B}\flat\text{Maj7(9,}\sharp\text{11,13)}}$	7.	$\dfrac{B\flat-}{\text{D}\flat\text{Maj6}}$	8.	$\dfrac{B}{\text{AMaj7(9,}\sharp\text{11,13)}}$
9.	$\dfrac{F-}{\text{G}\flat\text{Maj7(9,}\sharp\text{11)}}$	10.	$\dfrac{A\sharp-}{\text{BMaj7(9,}\sharp\text{11)}}$	11.	$\dfrac{D-}{\text{FMaj6}}$	12.	$\dfrac{G\flat}{\text{C}\flat\text{Maj7(9)}}$
13.	$\dfrac{A}{\text{DMaj7(9)}}$	14.	$\dfrac{A}{\text{GMaj7(9,}\sharp\text{11,13)}}$	15.	$\dfrac{A-}{\text{B}\flat\text{Maj7(9,}\sharp\text{11)}}$	16.	$\dfrac{F-}{\text{F}\sharp\text{Maj7(9,}\sharp\text{11)}}$
17.	$\dfrac{E}{\text{AMaj7(9)}}$	18.	$\dfrac{B-}{\text{DMaj6}}$	19.	$\dfrac{B\flat}{\text{E}\flat\text{Maj7(9)}}$	20	$\dfrac{B-}{\text{CMaj7(9,}\sharp\text{11)}}$

Practice 2.2. UST Recognition Practice for Dominant 7

1.	$\dfrac{E-}{\text{A7(9)}}$	2.	$\dfrac{C\sharp-D\sharp-}{\text{F}\sharp\text{7(9,13)}}$	3.	$\dfrac{B}{\text{D}\flat\text{7sus4(9,11)}}$	4.	$\dfrac{F\sharp-}{\text{E7sus4(9,11,13)}}$
5.	$\dfrac{G\flat}{\text{A}\flat\text{7sus4(9,11)}}$	6.	$\dfrac{C-D-}{\text{F7(9,13)}}$	7.	$\dfrac{G-}{\text{C7(9)}}$	8.	$\dfrac{G-}{\text{B}\flat\text{7(13)}}$
9.	$\dfrac{B\flat-}{\text{D}\flat\text{7sus4(10,13)}}$	10.	$\dfrac{B-}{\text{E7(9)}}$	11.	$\dfrac{C\sharp-}{\text{B7sus4(9,11,13)}}$	12.	$\dfrac{D-}{\text{F7(13)}}$
13.	$\dfrac{B}{\text{C}\sharp\text{7sus4(9,11)}}$	14.	$\dfrac{B\flat-C-}{\text{E}\flat\text{7(9,13)}}$	15.	$\dfrac{D-}{\text{G7(9)}}$	16.	$\dfrac{B-}{\text{D7sus4(10, 13)}}$
17.	$\dfrac{D\flat-E\flat-}{\text{G}\flat\text{7(9,13)}}$	18.	$\dfrac{D-}{\text{C7sus4(9,11,13)}}$	19.	$\dfrac{E\flat-}{\text{A}\flat\text{7(9)}}$	20.	$\dfrac{D\flat}{\text{E}\flat\text{7sus4(9,11)}}$

Practice 3.2. UST Recognition Practice for Minor 7

1.	$\dfrac{\text{D\#-}}{\text{C\#-7(9,11, 13)}}$	2.	$\dfrac{\text{E\flat}}{\text{F-7(9,11)}}$	3.	$\dfrac{\text{D\flat-}}{\text{G\flat-7(9)}}$	4.	$\dfrac{\text{A\flat}}{\text{B\flat-7(9,11)}}$
5.	$\dfrac{\text{G-}}{\text{C-7(9)}}$	6.	$\dfrac{\text{F\#-}}{\text{E-7(9,11,13)}}$	7.	$\dfrac{\text{A\flat-}}{\text{G\flat-7(9,11,13)}}$	8.	$\dfrac{\text{D}}{\text{E-7(9,11)}}$
9.	$\dfrac{\text{F\#-}}{\text{B-7(9)}}$	10.	$\dfrac{\text{G\flat}}{\text{A\flat-7(9,11)}}$	11.	$\dfrac{\text{A-}}{\text{G-7(9,11,13)}}$	12.	$\dfrac{\text{A\flat-}}{\text{D\flat-7(9)}}$
13.	$\dfrac{\text{C\#-}}{\text{B-7(9,11,13)}}$	14.	$\dfrac{\text{B\flat-}}{\text{E\flat-7(9)}}$	15.	$\dfrac{\text{E}}{\text{F\#-7(9,11)}}$	16.	$\dfrac{\text{G}}{\text{A-7(9,11)}}$
17.	$\dfrac{\text{G-}}{\text{F-7(9,11,13)}}$	18.	$\dfrac{\text{F-}}{\text{B\flat-7(9)}}$	19.	$\dfrac{\text{C}}{\text{D-7(9,11)}}$	20.	$\dfrac{\text{E-}}{\text{A-7(9)}}$

Practice 3.6. Open-Position Voice Leading: Minor 7

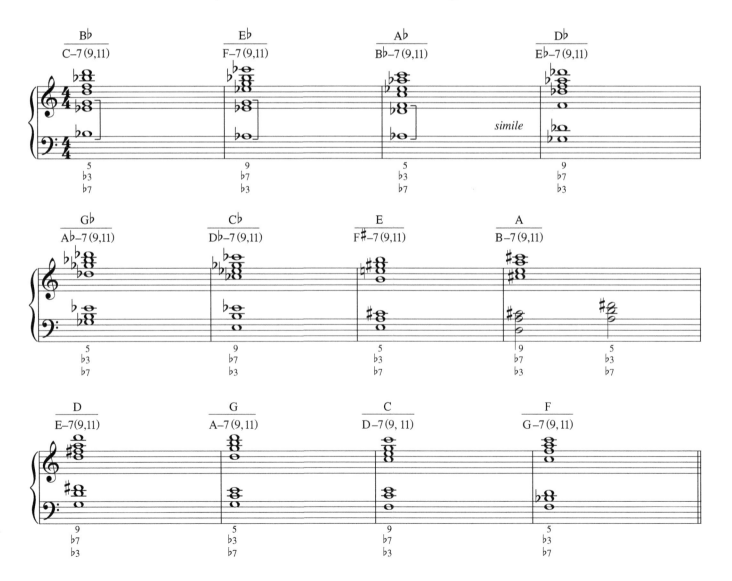

Practice 4.2. UST Recognition Practice for Minor 7♭5

1.	$\dfrac{\text{D}}{\text{E–7♭5(9,11)}}$	2.	$\dfrac{\text{G♭}}{\text{A♭–7♭5(9,11)}}$	3.	$\dfrac{\text{E♭ +5}}{\text{D♭–7♭5(9)}}$	4.	$\dfrac{\text{B +5}}{\text{A–7♭5(9)}}$
5.	$\dfrac{\text{B}}{\text{D♭–7♭5(9,11)}}$	6.	$\dfrac{\text{D♯ +5}}{\text{C♯–7♭5(9)}}$	7.	$\dfrac{\text{C}}{\text{D–7♭5(9,11)}}$	8.	$\dfrac{\text{F +5}}{\text{E♭–7♭5(9)}}$
9.	$\dfrac{\text{E}}{\text{F♯–7♭5(9,11)}}$	10.	$\dfrac{\text{A +5}}{\text{G–7♭5(9)}}$	11.	$\dfrac{\text{A♭}}{\text{B♭–7♭5(9,11)}}$	12.	$\dfrac{\text{A♭ +5}}{\text{G♭–7♭5(9)}}$
13.	$\dfrac{\text{C♯ +5}}{\text{B–7♭5(9)}}$	14.	$\dfrac{\text{E}}{\text{F♯–7♭5(9,11)}}$	15.	$\dfrac{\text{E +5}}{\text{D–7♭5(9)}}$	16.	$\dfrac{\text{B♭}}{\text{C–7♭5(9,11)}}$
17.	$\dfrac{\text{A +5}}{\text{G–7♭5(9)}}$	18.	$\dfrac{\text{A}}{\text{B–7♭5(9,11)}}$	19.	$\dfrac{\text{E♭}}{\text{F–7♭5(9,11)}}$	20.	$\dfrac{\text{B♭ +5}}{\text{A♭–7♭5(9)}}$

Practice 4.3. Minor 7♭5 LH Voicings

Practice 4.5. Open-Position Voice Leading: Minor 7♭5

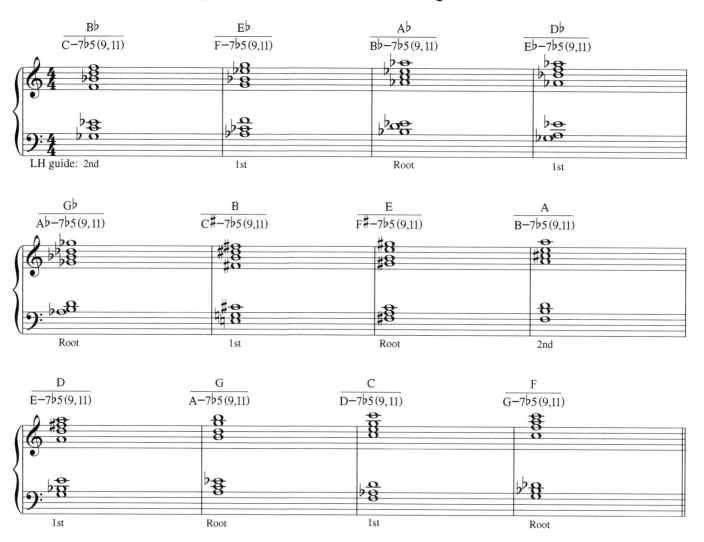

Practice 5.2. UST Recognition Practice for Diminished 7

1.	$\dfrac{B}{A°7(9)}$	2.	$\dfrac{F}{C°7(11)}$	3.	$\dfrac{D}{E♭°7(14)}$	4.	$\dfrac{E}{B°7(11)}$
5.	$\dfrac{C}{C♯°7(14)}$	6.	$\dfrac{B♭}{F°7(11)}$	7.	$\dfrac{A}{E°7(11)}$	8.	$\dfrac{G♯}{F♯°7(9)}$
9.	$\dfrac{A♭}{E♭°7(11)}$	10.	$\dfrac{A}{B♭°7(14)}$	11.	$\dfrac{A}{G°7(9)}$	12.	$\dfrac{E♭}{D♭°7(9)}$
13.	$\dfrac{C♯}{B°7(9)}$	14.	$\dfrac{F}{G♭°7(14)}$	15.	$\dfrac{C}{B♭°7(9)}$	16.	$\dfrac{D}{D♯°7(14)}$
17.	$\dfrac{B♭}{F°7(11)}$	18.	$\dfrac{E}{D°7(9)}$	19.	$\dfrac{D♭}{A♭°7(11)}$	20.	$\dfrac{B}{C°7(14)}$

Practice 5.3. Open-Position Voice Leading: Diminished 7

*Octave doubling of bottom note of UST optional

Practice 6.3. UST Recognition Practice for Altered Dominant

1. $\dfrac{\text{A♭-}}{\text{G7(♭9,♭13)}}$	2. $\dfrac{\text{G♭-}}{\text{E♭7(♯9,♯11)}}$	3. $\dfrac{\text{G}}{\text{C♯7(♭9,♯11)}}$	4. $\dfrac{\text{D♭}}{\text{F7(♯9,♭13)}}$
5. $\dfrac{\text{D♭-}}{\text{B♭7(♯9,♯11)}}$	6. $\dfrac{\text{A}}{\text{D♭7(♯9,♭13)}}$	7. $\dfrac{\text{E♭-}}{\text{D7(♭9,♭13)}}$	8. $\dfrac{\text{C}}{\text{F♯7(♭9,♯11)}}$
9. $\dfrac{\text{D♭-}}{\text{C7(♭9,♭13)}}$	10. $\dfrac{\text{A-}}{\text{G♭7(♯9,♯11)}}$	11. $\dfrac{\text{E♭}}{\text{A7(♭9,♯11)}}$	12. $\dfrac{\text{G}}{\text{B7(♯9,♭13)}}$
13. $\dfrac{\text{D}}{\text{A♭7(♭9,♯11)}}$	14. $\dfrac{\text{G-}}{\text{E7(♯9,♯11)}}$	15. $\dfrac{\text{G-}}{\text{F♯7(♭9,♭13)}}$	16. $\dfrac{\text{B}}{\text{E♭7(♯9,♭13)}}$
17. $\dfrac{\text{E♭-}}{\text{C7(♯9,♯11)}}$	18. $\dfrac{\text{B-}}{\text{B♭7(♭9,♭13)}}$	19. $\dfrac{\text{B♭}}{\text{E7(♭9,♯11)}}$	20. $\dfrac{\text{E-}}{\text{D♭7(♯9,♯11)}}$

Practice 6.4. UST Recognition Practice for Symmetrical Dominant

1. $\dfrac{\text{A}}{\text{C7}(\flat 9,13)}$	2. $\dfrac{\text{D-}}{\text{A}\flat 7(\flat 9,\sharp 11,13)}$	3. $\dfrac{\text{G}\sharp}{\text{B7}(\flat 9,13)}$	4. $\dfrac{\text{A-}}{\text{E}\flat 7(\flat 9,\sharp 11,13)}$
5. $\dfrac{\text{C}}{\text{E}\flat 7(\flat 9,13)}$	6. $\dfrac{\text{B}\flat}{\text{D}\flat 7(\flat 9,13)}$	7. $\dfrac{\text{F}\sharp}{\text{A7}(\flat 9,13)}$	8. $\dfrac{\text{B-}}{\text{F7}(\flat 9,\sharp 11,13)}$
9. $\dfrac{\text{C-}}{\text{F}\sharp 7(\flat 9,\sharp 11,13)}$	10. $\dfrac{\text{E-}}{\text{B}\flat 7(\flat 9,\sharp 11,13)}$	11. $\dfrac{\text{B}}{\text{D7}(\flat 9,13)}$	12. $\dfrac{\text{A}\sharp}{\text{C}\sharp 7(\flat 9,13)}$
13. $\dfrac{\text{B}\flat\text{-}}{\text{E7}(\flat 9,\sharp 11,13)}$	14. $\dfrac{\text{C-}}{\text{G}\flat 7(\flat 9,\sharp 11,13)}$	15. $\dfrac{\text{D}}{\text{F7}(\flat 9,13)}$	16. $\dfrac{\text{G}}{\text{B}\flat 7(\flat 9,13)}$
17. $\dfrac{\text{G-}}{\text{D}\flat 7(\flat 9,\sharp 11,13)}$	18. $\dfrac{\text{C}\sharp}{\text{E7}(\flat 9,13)}$	19. $\dfrac{\text{A}\flat\text{-}}{\text{D7}(\flat 9,\sharp 11,13)}$	20. $\dfrac{\text{E}}{\text{G7}(\flat 9,13)}$

Practice 6.6. Altered Dominant Voicings 1

Altered Dominant Voicings 2

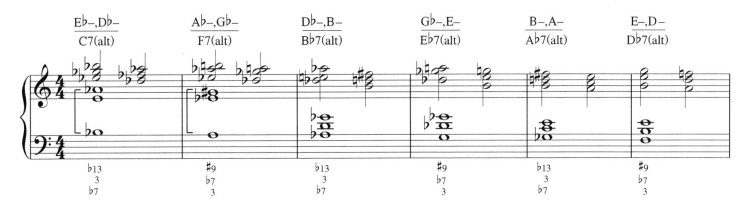

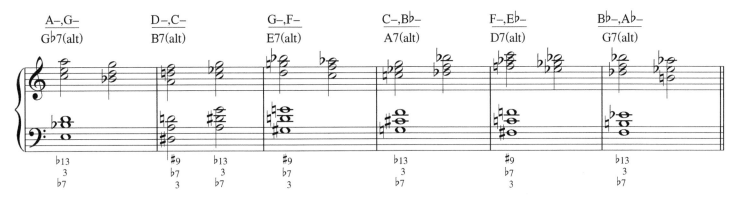

Practice 6.7. Symmetrical-Dominant Voicings 1

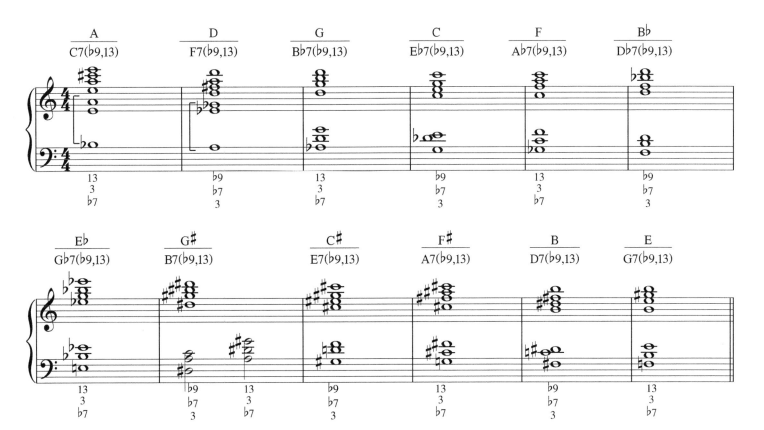

Symmetrical-Dominant Voicings 2

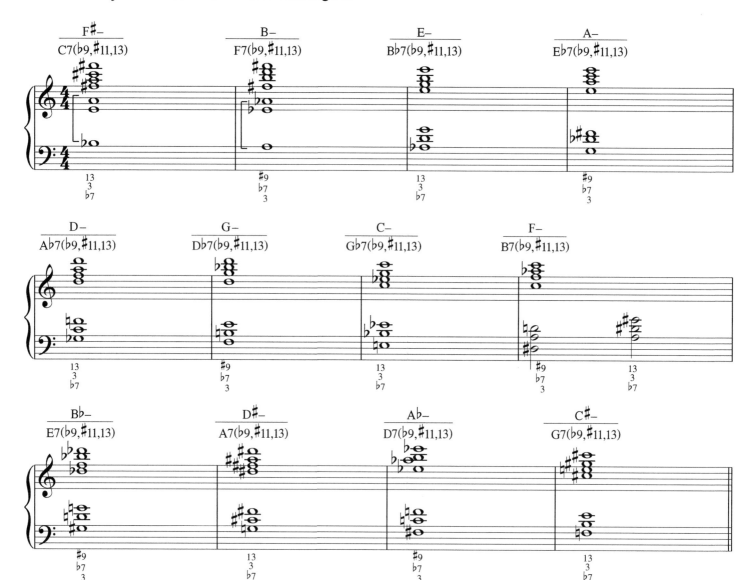

ABOUT THE AUTHOR

Photo by Portrait Simple

Suzanna Sifter is a professor in the piano department at Berklee College of Music. She has traveled extensively with Berklee to perform concerts and give master classes internationally in Europe, Asia, South America, and Canada. She holds a bachelor of music from Berklee College of Music and master's degree from New England Conservatory, having studied with Hal Crook, Herb Pomeroy, Dave Holland, and Charlie Banacos. Suzanna has performed with jazz greats John LaPorta and Alan Dawson. Her compositions have been featured on *In the Library* (D. Govoni) and *On the Edge* (T. Lada), where she was also featured on piano. Suzanna has three recordings as a leader, composer, and arranger: *Flowers for You* (1997), *Awakening* (2002), and *The Illumination* (2009).

More Fine Publications

GUITAR

BEBOP GUITAR SOLOS
by Michael Kaplan
00121703 Book $16.99

BLUES GUITAR TECHNIQUE
by Michael Williams
50449623 Book/Online Audio $27.99

BERKLEE GUITAR CHORD DICTIONARY
by Rick Peckham
50449546 Jazz – Book.........................$14.99
50449596 Rock – Book.........................$12.99

BERKLEE GUITAR STYLE STUDIES
by Jim Kelly
00200377 Book/Online Media...........$24.99

**CLASSICAL TECHNIQUE FOR THE
MODERN GUITARIST**
by Kim Perlak
00148781 Book/Online Audio..............$19.99

CONTEMPORARY JAZZ GUITAR SOLOS
by Michael Kaplan
00143596 Book.......................................$16.99

**CREATIVE CHORDAL HARMONY
FOR GUITAR**
by Mick Goodrick and Tim Miller
50449613 Book/Online Audio............$22.99

FUNK/R&B GUITAR
by Thaddeus Hogarth
50449569 Book/Online Audio............$19.99

GUITAR SWEEP PICKING
by Joe Stump
00151223 Book/Online Audio $19.99

INTRODUCTION TO JAZZ GUITAR
by Jane Miller
00125041 Book/Online Audio..............$22.99

**JAZZ GUITAR FRETBOARD
NAVIGATION**
by Mark White
00154107 Book/Online Audio..............$22.99

JAZZ SWING GUITAR
by Jon Wheatley
00139935 Book/Online Audio............$24.99

METAL GUITAR CHOP SHOP
by Joe Stump
50449601 Book/Online Audio $19.99

**A MODERN METHOD FOR GUITAR –
VOLUMES 1-3 COMPLETE***
by William Leavitt
00292990 Book/Online Media $49.99
*Individual volumes, media options, and
supporting songbooks available.*

**A MODERN METHOD FOR
GUITAR SCALES**
by Larry Baione
00199318 Book.......................................$14.99

READING STUDIES FOR GUITAR
by William Leavitt
50449490 Book... $17.99

Berklee Press publications feature material
developed at Berklee College of Music.
To browse the complete Berklee Press Catalog, go to
www.berkleepress.com

BASS

BERKLEE JAZZ BASS
by Rich Appleman, Whit Browne & Bruce Gertz
50449636 Book/Online Audio.......... $22.99

CHORD STUDIES FOR ELECTRIC BASS
by Rich Appleman & Joseph Viola
50449750 Book...................................... $17.99

FINGERSTYLE FUNK BASS LINES
by Joe Santerre
50449542 Book/Online Audio..............$19.99

FUNK BASS FILLS
by Anthony Vitti
50449608 Book/Online Audio $22.99

INSTANT BASS
by Danny Morris
50449502 Book/CD.................................. $9.99

METAL BASS LINES
by David Marvuglio
00122465 Book/Online Audio..............$19.99

**READING CONTEMPORARY
ELECTRIC BASS**
by Rich Appleman
50449770 Book......................................$22.99

ROCK BASS LINES
by Joe Santerre
50449478 Book/Online Audio...........$22.99

PIANO/KEYBOARD

BERKLEE JAZZ KEYBOARD HARMONY
by Suzanna Sifter
00138874 Book/Online Audio............$29.99

BERKLEE JAZZ PIANO
by Ray Santisi
50448047 Book/Online Audio $22.99

**BERKLEE JAZZ STANDARDS
FOR SOLO PIANO**
*arr. Robert Christopherson, Hey Rim Jeon,
Ross Ramsay, Tim Ray*
00160482 Book/Online Audio $19.99

**CHORD-SCALE IMPROVISATION
FOR KEYBOARD**
by Ross Ramsay
50449597 Book/CD $19.99

CONTEMPORARY PIANO TECHNIQUE
by Stephany Tiernan
50449545 Book/DVD............................$29.99

HAMMOND ORGAN COMPLETE
by Dave Limina
00237801 Book/Online Audio............$24.99

JAZZ PIANO COMPING
by Suzanne Davis
50449614 Book/Online Audio............$22.99

LATIN JAZZ PIANO IMPROVISATION
by Rebecca Cline
50449649 Book/Online Audio $29.99

PIANO ESSENTIALS
by Ross Ramsay
50448046 Book/Online Audio $24.99

SOLO JAZZ PIANO
by Neil Olmstead
50449641 Book/Online Audio...........$42.99

DRUMS

BEGINNING DJEMBE
by Michael Markus & Joe Galeota
00148210 Book/Online Video.............$16.99

BERKLEE JAZZ DRUMS
by Casey Scheuerell
50449612 Book/Online Audio............$24.99

DRUM SET WARM-UPS
by Rod Morgenstein
50449465 Book......................................$14.99

**A MANUAL FOR THE
MODERN DRUMMER**
by Alan Dawson & Don DeMichael
50449560 Book......................................$14.99

MASTERING THE ART OF BRUSHES
by Jon Hazilla
50449459 Book/Online Audio............$19.99

PHRASING
by Russ Gold
00120209 Book/Online Media $19.99

WORLD JAZZ DRUMMING
by Mark Walker
50449568 Book/CD................................$22.99

BERKLEE PRACTICE METHOD

GET YOUR BAND TOGETHER
With additional volumes for other instruments, plus
a teacher's guide.
Bass
*by Rich Appleman, John Repucci and the
Berklee Faculty*
50449427 Book/CD $24.99
Drum Set
*by Ron Savage, Casey Scheuerell and the
Berklee Faculty*
50449429 Book/CD $17.99
Guitar
by Larry Baione and the Berklee Faculty
50449426 Book/CD...............................$19.99
Keyboard
*by Russell Hoffmann, Paul Schmeling and
the Berklee Faculty*
50449428 Book/Online Audio............$19.99

VOICE

BELTING
by Jeannie Gagné
00124984 Book/Online Media............$22.99

THE CONTEMPORARY SINGER
by Anne Peckham
50449595 Book/Online Audio $27.99

JAZZ VOCAL IMPROVISATION
by Mili Bermejo
00159290 Book/Online Audio.............$19.99

TIPS FOR SINGERS
by Carolyn Wilkins
50449557 Book/CD $19.95

**VOCAL WORKOUTS FOR THE
CONTEMPORARY SINGER**
by Anne Peckham
50448044 Book/Online Audio..........$24.99

YOUR SINGING VOICE
by Jeannie Gagné
50449619 Book/Online Audio.............$29.99

WOODWINDS & BRASS

TRUMPET SOUND EFFECTS
by Craig Pederson & Ueli Dörig
00121626 Book/Online Audio.............$14.99

SAXOPHONE SOUND EFFECTS
by Ueli Dörig
50449628 Book/Online Audio...........$15.99

THE TECHNIQUE OF THE FLUTE
by Joseph Viola
00214012 Book...$19.99

STRINGS/ROOTS MUSIC

BERKLEE HARP
by Felice Pomeranz
00144263 Book/Online Audio...........$24.99

BEYOND BLUEGRASS BANJO
by Dave Hollander and Matt Glaser
50449610 Book/CD.................................$19.99

BEYOND BLUEGRASS MANDOLIN
by John McGann and Matt Glaser
50449609 Book/CD $19.99

BLUEGRASS FIDDLE & BEYOND
by Matt Glaser
50449602 Book/CD.................................$19.99

CONTEMPORARY CELLO ETUDES
by Mike Block
00159292 Book/Online Audio............$19.99

EXPLORING CLASSICAL MANDOLIN
by August Watters
00125040 Book/Online Media..........$24.99

THE IRISH CELLO BOOK
by Liz Davis Maxfield
50449652 Book/Online Audio.......... $27.99

JAZZ UKULELE
by Abe Lagrimas, Jr.
00121624 Book/Online Audio............$22.99

WELLNESS

MANAGE YOUR STRESS AND PAIN THROUGH MUSIC
by Dr. Suzanne B. Hanser and
Dr. Susan E. Mandel
50449592 Book/CD $34.99

MUSICIAN'S YOGA
by Mia Olson
50449587 Book $19.99

NEW MUSIC THERAPIST'S HANDBOOK
by Dr. Suzanne B. Hanser
00279325 Book..$29.99

MUSIC PRODUCTION & ENGINEERING

AUDIO MASTERING
by Jonathan Wyner
50449581 Book/CD..............................$29.99

AUDIO POST PRODUCTION
by Mark Cross
50449627 Book $19.99

CREATING COMMERCIAL MUSIC
by Peter Bell
00278535 Book/Online Media...........$19.99

THE SINGER-SONGWRITER'S GUIDE TO RECORDING IN THE HOME STUDIO
by Shane Adams
00148211 Book.......................................$19.99

UNDERSTANDING AUDIO
by Daniel M. Thompson
00148197 Book.......................................$42.99

MUSIC BUSINESS

CROWDFUNDING FOR MUSICIANS
by Laser Malena-Webber
00285092 Book...................................... $17.99

ENGAGING THE CONCERT AUDIENCE
by David Wallace
00244532 Book/Online Media..........$16.99

HOW TO GET A JOB IN THE MUSIC INDUSTRY
by Keith Hatschek with Breanne Beseda
00130699 Book $27.99

MAKING MUSIC MAKE MONEY
by Eric Beall
00355740 Book $29.99

MUSIC INDUSTRY FORMS
by Jonathan Feist
00121814 Book $16.99

MUSIC LAW IN THE DIGITAL AGE
by Allen Bargfrede
00366048 Book $24.99

MUSIC MARKETING
by Mike King
50449588 Book $24.99

PROJECT MANAGEMENT FOR MUSICIANS
by Jonathan Feist
50449659 Book...................................... $34.99

THE SELF-PROMOTING MUSICIAN
by Peter Spellman
00119607 Book......................................$29.99

CONDUCTING

CONDUCTING MUSIC TODAY
by Bruce Hangen
00237719 Book/Online Media...........$24.99

MUSIC THEORY & EAR TRAINING

BEGINNING EAR TRAINING
by Gilson Schachnik
50449548 Book/Online Audio........... $17.99

BERKLEE CONTEMPORARY MUSIC NOTATION
by Jonathan Feist
00202547 Book $24.99

BERKLEE MUSIC THEORY
by Paul Schmeling
50449615 Book 1/Online Audio........$24.99
50449616 Book 2/Online Audio.......$24.99

CONTEMPORARY COUNTERPOINT
by Beth Denisch
00147050 Book/Online Audio $24.99

MUSIC NOTATION
by Mark McGrain
50449399 Book......................................$24.99
by Matthew Nicholl & Richard Grudzinski
50449540 Book.....................................$24.99

REHARMONIZATION TECHNIQUES
by Randy Felts
50449496 Book......................................$29.99

SONGWRITING/COMPOSING

BEGINNING SONGWRITING
by Andrea Stolpe with Jan Stolpe
00138503 Book/Online Audio...........$22.99

COMPLETE GUIDE TO FILM SCORING
by Richard Davis
50449607 Book $34.99

THE CRAFT OF SONGWRITING
by Scarlet Keys
00159283 Book/Online Audio...........$22.99

CREATIVE STRATEGIES IN FILM SCORING
by Ben Newhouse
00242911 Book/Online Media............ $27.99

JAZZ COMPOSITION
by Ted Pease
50448000 Book/Online Audio $39.99

MELODY IN SONGWRITING
by Jack Perricone
50449419 Book.....................................$24.99

MUSIC COMPOSITION FOR FILM AND TELEVISION
by Lalo Schifrin
50449604 Book.....................................$39.99

POPULAR LYRIC WRITING
by Andrea Stolpe
50449553 Book $16.99

THE SONGWRITER'S WORKSHOP
by Jimmy Kachulis
Harmony
50449519 Book/Online Audio $29.99
Melody
50449518 Book/Online Audio $24.99

SONGWRITING: ESSENTIAL GUIDE
by Pat Pattison
Lyric Form and Structure
50481582 Book.....................................$19.99
Rhyming
00124366 Book......................................$22.99

SONGWRITING IN PRACTICE
by Mark Simos
00244545 Book.....................................$16.99

SONGWRITING STRATEGIES
by Mark Simos
50449621 Book $24.99

ARRANGING & IMPROVISATION

ARRANGING FOR HORNS
by Jerry Gates
00121625 Book/Online Audio............$22.99

BERKLEE BOOK OF JAZZ HARMONY
by Joe Mulholland & Tom Hojnacki
00113755 Book/Online Audio $29.99

IMPROVISATION FOR CLASSICAL MUSICIANS
by Eugene Friesen with Wendy M. Friesen
50449637 Book/CD $24.99

MODERN JAZZ VOICINGS
by Ted Pease and Ken Pullig
50449485 Book/Online Audio..........$24.99

AUTOBIOGRAPHY

LEARNING TO LISTEN: THE JAZZ JOURNEY OF GARY BURTON
by Gary Burton
00117798 Book...................................... $34.99

Prices subject to change without notice. Visit your local
music dealer or bookstore, or go to **www.berkleepress.com**

STUDY THE BERKLEE PIANO METHOD ONLINE

Develop your piano technique and gain a greater command of the keyboard in a variety of musical styles including blues, rock, and jazz.

Visit **online.berklee.edu** to

- Download a free piano handbook

- Watch video clinics with industry professionals

- Explore a free sample lesson from an online 12-week course

 Berklee Online

1-866-BERKLEE